SPARKS OF CONNECTION

SPARKS OF CONNECTION

MATCHBOOK MOMENTS

ROZELLE WRITERS GUILD

RWG Wordsmiths

For Ron Rozelle, our writing teacher.
Thank you for your guidance and inspiration.

Contents

Foreword

During a visit to my mother-in-law's, she inquired whether I needed any matches. Thinking it was never a bad thing to have plenty of them around and accustomed to her offers of freebies as she decluttered her house, I accepted her offer. Much to my surprise, she returned a moment later, not with a few matchbooks, but rather with an entire shopping bag full!

As I went through the stash, grabbing one to light candles, start the fireplace, or ignite the grill, I became intrigued by the tokens. Their varied covers were snippets of the places that my in-law's family had lived and visited. Companies where my father-in-law had been employed, restaurants where the family had dined, banks where they had done business, places they had vacationed...all of these represented a snapshot of their experiences. Physical reminders in the form of shiny covers, bold print, and varying textures captured fragments of the towns and states they resided and the places they traveled. This diverse conglomeration made a map of the past that marked the places and seasons of their lives.

Some of them were fun reminders that could make you envy the moment, such as a wedding favor or a footlong matchbook from a national park. Other matches were mysterious: shiny gold covers with blank insides, the name of a shop without a location, a political campaign for local sheriff. Even the matches themselves had their own personality. Wooden sticks, combustible ignition sources in an array of colors, and of course, traditional red tips on cardboard awaited the opportunity to provide a flame.

As I sifted through them, I tried to imagine the moment the book had been collected. Had it been a Sunday dinner out? Was it a business trip? What could the story be behind this piece of the past? A thought occurred to me. Wouldn't it be fun to write short stories using the match collection as inspiration? The Rozelle Writer's Guild was looking for a project we could do together. This was perfect. Each of us could write some prose or poetry using the information from one or two of the matchbooks and fold it into an anthology for others to enjoy.

This book is our collection of stories and poems inspired by the footprints of a family's journey in life. Enjoy!

Diana Reckart

Sparks of Connection

Matchbook Moments

Life's Possibilities
inspired by
Small Mementos

Jeremiah's Greenhouse

LYNNETTE BROOKS

When we were young, we followed the sun.
All of life was before us.
With children yet to come, freedom had no boundaries.
Weekends and holidays were ours to do with as we pleased.
Along the way, we were to become seekers of adventure.

A new restaurant or park.
Who knew what would capture our imaginations?
Love paved each path we trod;
laughter wove the strings of our hearts.

There was no "getting lost" involved;
we had no destination.
Prowling the edges of our hometown,
We were drawn to a multitude of places.

Friends suggested we buy a camera
and take pictures to document our trips.
Why, we asked?
We always got a matchbook to mark the occasion.

One such place we found was known by many:
Jeremiah's Greenhouse.
A bit rustic and remote, service was iffy.
Tables had been placed between gorgeous old oaks.
Pergolas were draped with lightly scented, blooming green-
ery.

Neither remembers the menu nor price;
a photo would not suffice.
Our Matchbook Collection would remind us
of name and location.

We had traveled and memories were made.
Neither distance nor time were ever a factor.
Us. Bob and Earlene.
Together, we followed the Sun.

Spats

CORINNA SEE

Slick city streets gleamed beneath lamplight, and Josie struggled to keep up with her mother's quick steps as Mrs. Duchannes skirted puddles, petticoats swishing around kidskin button boots.

"Come along, Josephine," she admonished. "The hour is late."

Genevieve Duchannes prided herself on never being late. Try as she might to instill such conventions, her daughter had not yet mastered the art of punctuality—nor of propriety. Genevieve's chocolate silk gown was perfectly tailored to her slim figure, tastefully trimmed in delicate lace, and spotless even as she swept over the damp sidewalk in her haste. The way Genevieve's manicure tightened around Josie's small gloved hand as they hurried, perfectly rouged lips set in a firm line, Josie knew that her mother regretted not having sent for a cab before they left the department store. But the evening fitting had taken longer than planned for, and Chicago's streets had all but emptied as soon as the storm blew through.

For all her dishevelment, Josie might have blown around with it. Her hat sat askew atop her unruly dark curls. One shoe was not buttoned properly. A spot of red jam colored the edge of her petticoat, where Josie had thoughtlessly wiped her sticky fingers after the department store clerk offered a tart.

Genevieve missed nothing, and Josie had realized as soon as she'd done it that her mother had seen. She'd looked up from her chair to where Genevieve stood, statuesque, while the dressmaker draped and pinned folds of silk; Josie's eyes met her mother's in the looking-glass, and though Genevieve's gaze was impassive, Josie wanted to shrink and hide behind those folds.

Though the incident had not been mentioned, she knew it would be. Josie waited for it, and that wait seemed even heavier a burden than the weight of her mother's disapproval.

Mercifully, Genevieve chose this moment to address it.

"You will have Grete take that petticoat and work on the stain. Then you will go straight to sleep." Genevieve's tone was crisp, and Josie knew better than to offer any response.

"Honestly, Josephine. Seven years old and you still have yet to learn to carry your handkerchief. We shall have to increase your etiquette lessons."

Soon as they rounded the corner, Josie blinked against the sudden wash of garish marquee lighting, while a cacophony of music and raucous laughter swallowed Genevieve's lecture.

"Oh, oh," Genevieve muttered. "The theater district at this hour, I didn't think—"

"Mama!" Josie's eyes were wide as she swiveled her head, twisting away from her mother's firm grip on her hand to take in as much as she could.

Never before had she seen this street after dark. During the day, the doorways were dark and the windows were curtained. People hurried by on their way to mundane destinations. Josie had just occasionally traversed the way by the light of day, her hand encased in her mother's or father's. Never before had she seen it so *alive*.

Doors stood open, sentry to the men and women who passed through. More men, all sharply dressed, and women in skirts with progressively shorter hemlines thronged gaily on the sidewalks, peeking through windows with curtains drawn back to reveal plush lounges made hazy with the smoke of cigars and more fashionable cigarettes.

"Mama, wait! I want to see!"

Without response, Genevieve only yanked Josie along, increasingly impatient as she was forced to slow their pace to weave through the crowd.

Josie attempted to plant her feet and pull back, to no avail as Genevieve's determination drove her forward. Instead, she had to follow her mother, stumbling in her distraction as she peered around the slim waists and suit pants that stood between her and the questionable establishments.

Genevieve muttered something else that Josie could not hear over the din of the crowd's raucous laughter—squeals of delighted indignation as women teased men, who feigned disapproval. Faint notes of music floated through the haze of cigarette smoke and Josie struggled not to cough; the acridity was sharply tanged with alcohol, but underneath that, hints of perfumes and colognes, and something else she could only imagine to be some kind of sinful indulgence.

The further they moved through the crowd, the closer they weaved toward the entrances that lined the broad walk. Josie craned her neck to peer further inside, past a dark smog of smoke to brightly lit stages. There, she could glimpse ladies in slinky, beaded attire that sparkled in a playful flirtation with the voices of vaudeville: rich, soulful tones of saxophone interspersed with a lighter dance of piano keys. Such notes blended with a chorus of other instruments she was unable to discern, try as she might.

She closed her eyes, trying harder.

"*Oof!*" Josie lurched to the side then, having collided with something large and soft stepping out of one doorway. She stopped where she stood and looked up, up—past an ample belly in a plaid waistcoat to dark eyes in a broad face, frowning down at her from beneath a heavy brow. An unlit cigar dangled from the corner of the man's mouth.

"Josephine!" Genevieve reproved, further tightening her grip on Josie's hand. "Come *along*." She bent her head toward her daughter and lowered her voice. "This is no place for a lady."

"Lady!"

The gruff voice stopped Josie from taking a step, and she stood, brown eyes transfixed on the man.

"Lady," he drawled more slowly this time, and while she knew he addressed Genevieve, he still looked at Josie.

He gestured to his cigar with one meaty hand. "Ya got a light?"

Mrs. Duchannes straightened herself to her full height, towering over Josie's small stature, and looked down her nose at the man—though she was hardly taller than he.

"Certainly, sir, I do not!" she replied in her primmest tone. She fixed him with a frosty glare that demanded to know how he might have thought up such an inconceivable notion.

He shrugged his thick shoulders. "Just askin' is all."

"Mr. Spates! Mr. Spates!"

In the doorway behind him, a young woman clad in a fiery red number that did not reach her bare knees, appeared below the sign that only just caught Josie's attention: SPATS: THE ALL TIME GOOD TIME GOOD DRINKS AND DANCE HALL.

"Mr. Spates, your saxophonist is getting handsy again!" the girl complained. She stamped her foot and folded her arms beneath sequined cleavage; from one hand dangled a huge fan of billowing feathers. Josie's eyes widened and she reached out, wanting to feel the soft plumes between her fingers.

The man called Spates only responded to the complaints with a grunt, to which the girl huffed. Then she uncrossed her arms and bit down on her bottom lip, widening her eyes.

"And Mr. Capone would like a *word*," she added quietly.

With another grunt, Spates turned around and headed back inside, and Josie looked up at her mother, who only watched the pair disappear into the shadows, scandalized.

This unsettled Josie; never before had she seen her mother rendered speechless.

"Mama," she said, desperate to elicit some sort of response. "May I have a fan like that?"

Genevieve shook off her stupor and turned cold gray eyes to her daughter.

"Learn this well, Josephine," she lectured. "This is *no place* for the likes of us." She raised her chin, and only just loosened her grasp on her daughter's hand. "Now let's go."

She turned on the toe of her shoe and began walking. Josie hurried to keep pace.

"Mama, what did he mean when he asked about a light?"

Caught off guard once again, Genevieve stopped underneath the glow of a streetlight.

"Josephine, that man assumed that I..." She shuddered. "That I *smoke*. Let that be another lesson for you: nice girls—*ladies*—do not carry matches because they do not smoke. Do you understand?"

"Yes, Mama."

* * *

"I understand *perfectly*." Josie puckered up and blew a kiss to the photo stuck to the corner of her dressing table mirror. "Thank you, Mama."

Genevieve's likeness only stared in response, and Josie imagined the icy look in her mother's gray eyes—the color discernible from the rest of the black and white shades—was a reproof for the scarlet shade she'd painted her lips. Or, perhaps, it could be admonishment for any one of many things, she supposed.

Well. Showtime. She stood, reaching for her feathers.

"Josie! Ya got a light?"

Josie leaned into the mirror and applied another coat of lipstick. "Honestly, Mr. Spates, where in this getup do you think I might keep a match?" She ran her fingers through her curls, tousling them even more so they spilled enticingly over her bare shoulders.

"Dunno, girlie, but ya always seem to have one on ya!" He looked her up and down, giving a single nod of approval before turning his gaze to her cluttered dressing table. "I know you stole another matchbook from my office, Josie! Along with a bottle of moonshine; that'll come out of your wages, missy." Mr. Spates removed the unlit cigar from his mouth and examined it thoughtfully. "Prohibition." He spat out the word, and then waggled a thick finger at her. "Now! Where do ya keep your cigarettes?"

Josie fixed him with a saccharine smile. "If there's anything my mother taught me, Mr. Spates, it's that nice girls do not carry matches because nice girls do not smoke."

He brought bushy eyebrows together, and she anticipated a question about whether she considered herself a nice girl, until the piano summoned her to the stage. Josie retrieved her fan and brushed the plumes over her blushed cheek.

"If you'll excuse me, Mr. Spates, I believe I have a performance to give."

He twisted his lips into a grimace of a response, cigar dangling unlit from one corner while he waited expectantly. Josie smirked, plucking a single match from her cleavage.

Twirling it between painted fingernails, she handed it over as she and her feathers sashayed toward the stage.

Humphrey's Oasis

KATHY SIMS

It wasn't the humidity; it was the heat. Desiccating, bake-your-buns heat. Jamie was sure if she stood still too long, the soles of her tennis shoes would melt into the street. Her gauzy floral blouse and white capris were usually comfortable, even in direct sun, but today, fear had her sweating profusely. Her clothes felt like clammy hands clinging to her. Despite this, she looked fresh and dry since the moisture evaporated as fast as it formed. The bus stop on the corner in front of the strip mall had an awning that offered a patch of shade, but the instructions she'd been given were to wait at the curb. Without knowing who or what to expect, she didn't dare risk deviating from the orders. Shielding her eyes, she looked up and down the street, clutching her shoulder bag tightly to her side.

A rude honk from behind startled her, and she spun around as a rattling, dusty truck pulled up beside her. Whatever its original color, years of baking in the desert sun had degraded it. Probably once a proud, powerful fire engine red, the rusty orange truck now looked like it was coated in

Cheeto dust. Although pitted and flaking, the chrome trim still shone in places, reflecting the rays of the overhead sun like light sabers into her eyes.

Blinking, Jamie peered in the open window of the truck as it rolled to a stop beside her. The interior was dark as her eyes struggled to adjust from the bright, glaring sun.

"Get in." The voice was firm, deep, and male.

A sudden chill rolled through her, raising goose bumps on her hot arms. She did not want to do this, but what choice did she have? The driver reached across the cab and shoved open the door, which groaned reluctantly like an old man getting out of a chair. He pulled a well-worn but well-cared for cowboy hat closer to him, making room on the bench seat. Gingerly, she perched on the scorching cracked leather, grateful her pants offered some protection, although her thin blouse gave none. Jamie winced and inched forward on the seat to lift her body off the backrest. She pulled the door shut, tucking her purse on the edge of the seat between her and the door, but before she had a chance to buckle up, the truck accelerated forward, then lurched into a hard right turn. Jamie hung onto the door's armrest to keep from sliding across the seat and crushing his hat. She didn't think he'd appreciate that.

Without looking away from the street before him, he asked cryptically, "Do you have it?"

She studied him. Shaggy brown hair pushed behind his ears revealed a clean-shaven jaw and a blunt nose. His hair brushed the collar of a faded pearl snap shirt and his well-worn jeans were tucked into brown boots. Lean, strong, quiet. A classic cowboy. He should have been one of the good guys.

"Well?" His glance was cold, and his tone irritated.

Nervous and nauseous, all she could do was nod. The scorching air blasting in through the window was tangling her hair into a thousand knots. She looked for a button to push, but there was only a window crank missing its knob. She reached down to try and turn it anyway, to close the window at least partially.

"Doesn't work." He was still staring at the road but was very much aware of what she was doing.

Jamie sat back and tried to gather her hair into a hand-held ponytail. The truck changed lanes abruptly, and she slid on the seat. With a little squeak, she dropped her hair and grabbed the arm rest again.

The driver's lips curled in a slight smile.

"Relax, Mouse. Nothing's going to happen until we get there."

Another strong shiver shook her. "Where?"

"Humphrey's Oasis." He looked at her. His face was hard and his brown eyes cold as stone. "Sit back, shut up, enjoy the ride."

Jamie clung to the truck door as if her life depended on it. A dry swallow did nothing to ease her tight throat. She turned away from him and watched the passing scenery change from suburbs to desert.

Trying to distract her thoughts from the quiet cowboy, she made another attempt to corral her hair. Between the hot leather and the sweltering wind, she was sweating plenty and her blouse was sticking to the seat. Why would anyone keep a truck with no air conditioning in this climate? You would think even a cowboy could afford a better ride.

What had she gotten herself mixed up in? No, what had *Trixie* done that had sucked them both into this ugly, dangerous mess? Riding through the desert to an unknown destination with a strange man, carrying an envelope holding who knows what to rescue her dearest friend, who was captive somewhere.

It had started on Friday night with what was supposed to be a simple celebration of Jamie's birthday. No party, no pressure—just her and Trixie enjoying Tex-Mex and conversation. Jamie had gone home after a second margarita because she'd promised to help a friend move bright and early Saturday morning. Trixie wanted to go clubbing, grab a few drinks, flirt, do a little dancing, and maybe even meet Mr. Right.

"The night is still young!" she'd protested, "It's your birthday!" Jamie had stuck to her guns. She didn't like breaking promises.

"Fine," Trixie had flounced away. "Tomorrow night, I'll tell you about the great time I had without you."

Instead, Saturday afternoon had brought a small package to Jamie's doorstep. Inside was a mailbox key, typed directions, and a gruesome gift. Trixie's cold pinky finger, the nail painted gloss black with a tiny rhinestone jewel. Jamie had almost thrown up when she saw it. The message had been crystal clear. NO POLICE. If Jamie went to the authorities or spoke to anyone about what was happening, there'd be another little package with another little present. Truly terrified, she'd dutifully complied with the instructions, naively believing whoever had her friend would keep their word.

She was so dumb. She shouldn't be here. She should have called the cops and let them handle this. She'd already blown it. She'd thrown away whatever leverage she gained from picking up the manila envelope at the post office box when she'd gotten in the truck.

"What's going to happen now?" The question slipped from her brain to her lips before she could stop it.

Cowboy stared straight ahead and said nothing.

She took a deep breath. As frightened as she was, Jamie was now Trixie's only hope. She had to be brave. She *had* to. For Trixie, her best friend. Her sister.

* * *

After what must have been at least an hour, Cowboy turned off the main road and onto a gravel drive heading west into the desert hills. As the bumps and ruts got rougher, Jamie gave up once again on her hair and clung to the door. When the road curved around to the back of the first foothill, a small cluster of weathered, gray buildings appeared, grouped around the edge of a circular dirt expanse at the end of the driveway. The ranch hunkered at the base of the mountains.

There was a corral attached to what was once a red barn that had rails missing and posts leaning drunkenly towards the ground. Opposite the corral stood a slightly newer, but still weathered, two-story building with a large porch. Rows of windows on the second floor gave it the appearance of a rustic dormitory. Cowboy pulled up and parked at the center structure, a long low building with another full-length porch and railings that looked like they should have horses tied to them. There were no other vehicles in sight.

"Get out." Grabbing his hat, Cowboy slid out his door and settled it on his head in a smooth, practiced move. As he came around the front of the truck, Jamie hurriedly pushed open the door and climbed out. He reached for her arm, but she stepped away, wrapping her arms defensively around her purse, clutching it to her chest.

"Inside." He stepped back, hands held up, obviously intending for her to go first.

"Where's my sister?"

Good job, Jamie, she thought. *Nice time to make a stand, out here in the middle of nowhere with a guy who could probably pick you up and carry you anywhere he wanted.* She flushed, uncomfortably aware that in other circumstances, she might like this stern cowboy to do exactly that. A sudden flashback to the cold pinky lying in a bed of cotton derailed that tempting train of thought. *Focus, idiot! This is not one of Trixie's bodice-ripping romance novels.*

Cowboy looked her up and down, then he shrugged.

"Suit yourself. I'm going inside where there's air conditioning and getting something cold to drink." He stepped to the porch.

"Wait. I didn't come here for a cold drink. I came to get my sister."

He paused and looked back at her. "She's not here yet," he said and disappeared through the door.

Flummoxed, Jamie gazed at her surroundings. This was getting weirder and scarier by the minute. The desert was quiet except for the ticking of the truck's engine cooling. She rubbed her arms, disgusted by the dust coating her sweaty face and body. Her hair was a bird's nest of tangles from the wind. She was hot, thirsty, and needed to pee. It was the last item that made her square her shoulders and step up on the porch. As she pushed the door open, she noticed the window was etched with the word "Oasis" above silhouettes of a palm tree and a camel in dunes. "Oasis," she muttered. "Huh."

Blessed cool air kissed her cheeks as Jamie stepped into a large great room. Through an open archway to the right, she could see a kitchen. Cowboy's Stetson was sitting upside down on the kitchen table, visible through the doorway. Directly opposite the front door was a hallway and to the left, a large stone fireplace anchored the living room. Decorated in traditional dude ranch style, a grouping of oversized brown leather furniture faced the fireplace. A coffee table made from a highly polished cross-section of a tree was centered beneath a deer antler chandelier, with a bowl of matches, an agate ashtray, and some magazines across it. Jamie could hear sounds from the kitchen and assumed it was the cowboy fixing his drink. She darted across the room into the hall.

A door ajar at the end of the hallway revealed a bathroom. She wanted to investigate the closed rooms she passed, but her bladder wouldn't wait.

It was a relief to get her needs taken care of, and splash the sweaty dirt off her arms and face. She looked at herself in the mirror and ran her fingers through her hair, but it was hopeless. She looked like a ball of dandelion fluff. *Who cares?* she told herself sternly. *This is a rescue mission, not a social soiree.*

Irritated with the errant images of a wild west romance flickering in the corners of her mind, Jamie yanked open the door and ran smack into Cowboy's chest.

Startled and embarrassed, she coalesced her feelings into fury and focused it on him.

"What are you doing? Listening? There's no window in there, I can't escape," she snarled.

He held out a glass of ice water. "I thought you might like something to drink."

She snatched it out of his hand and pushed past him. She wouldn't be able to check those closed doors now.

Jamie stomped into the living room and threw herself into an overstuffed chair. The seat deflated unexpectedly beneath her, and her butt landed with a solid thump on the support slats of the chair. The abrupt drop picked her feet off the ground, and her arms flew out in an unconscious response to catch herself. The water spilled out of her glass, a chilly cascade down the front of her shirt and capris. Jamie jerked herself back to her feet as the cold shocked her skin and ice cubes clattered to the floor.

"Crap," she muttered, brushing futilely at her clothes. Her sheer blouse was pasted to her chest and stomach, highlighting the lines of her bra and the shadow of her naval. The puddle spot left on her lap made it look like she had wet her pants.

A choking sound caused her to glance up. Cowboy, leaning against the frame of the hallway, red-faced, shoulders shaking. Catching her glare, a guffaw burst from his lips and he sagged against the wall, chortling.

"Hoo-wee, that was the funniest thing I've seen in months." He wiped his sleeve across his eyes. "What do you do for an encore?"

Jamie's angry retort was cut off by the sound of an engine pulling up in front of the house. Her heart began to pound, and her stomach rolled, queasy with fear.

Cowboy straightened up, suddenly serious. He set his glass on the coffee table and crossed the room to stand by the entryway. Jamie drifted over to the windows looking out on the porch, trying to get a clue as to what was happening.

Outside, a dusty black sedan had parked next to the truck. Two men in suits and black Ray-Ban sunglasses got out of the front seat. The man on the passenger side opened the rear door. Jamie held her breath, heart racing, hoping. A shaggy blonde head appeared above the door. Trixie!

Jamie started for the door, only to find her way blocked by Cowboy.

"Let me go! I want to see my sister."

He shook his head and pointed to the chair she'd wet herself in. "Sit. Wait."

Jamie opened her mouth to argue, but he grabbed her shoulders, spun her around, and shoved her towards the chair. "Sit down."

Shaken by the rough handling, Jamie sat, tucking her precious purse behind her back as she gingerly settled into the duplicitous chair. She fixed her eyes on the glass bowl of souvenir matchbooks on the coffee table, trying to calm her pounding heart. "Breathe," she told herself. She stared at the image the matchbooks bore, the same image that was on the door, as her centering point. Her heart calmed.

Cowboy stood by the side of the chair and they waited.

The door banged open, rattling the etched window. The three passengers came in: Suit, Trixie, Suit. The second Suit, wearing an oversized bright red tie, had a firm grip on Trixie's elbow. Her head was down, hair blocking her face. Her feet shuffled like she was exhausted. She still wore the scoop neck black glitter top and tight black leather pants from Friday night. Red Tie steered Trixie to the sofa across the room from Jamie, where she plopped down wearily, eyes on her shoes, her hands tucked under her arms. He dropped like a rock beside her, while the other man, wearing a blue tie, stood like a guard at the end of the couch. Frozen like figures in a diorama, the two groups assessed the situation.

How had the world turned upside down in just twenty-four hours? Instead of curled up on her bed reading, Jamie was sitting in a broken chair, in wet clothes with an envelope, and its unknown contents hidden behind her. She stared at her sister and the dangerous men around them.

Jamie's eyes narrowed as she studied Trixie. She'd picked up a matchbook from a bowl and was nervously flipping the cover open, then sliding it shut. Jamie frowned. There was no bandage on either of her hands. What was going on? Jamie shifted in the uncomfortable chair and Trixie looked up.

"Jamie!" Trixie moved as if to stand, but Red Tie put a hand on her leg, and she subsided. Her eyes widened at Jamie, like she was trying to communicate something.

"What's going on?" Jamie surprised herself by how confident and assured her voice sounded.

Blue Tie, the one who had been driving, took off his sunglasses. "She doing the talking for you?" he asked Cowboy.

"Nope."

"Then shut her up," he sneered at Jamie. Tucking his sunglasses inside his jacket, Blue Tie assumed a professional air. "Gentlemen, shall we get down to business?"

He looked at Cowboy. "Do you have the envelope?"

Cowboy nodded.

"Let's see it."

Cowboy looked down at Jamie expectantly. She glanced at all the faces in the room, unreadable. Even Trixie's, a face she knew as well as her own, held an expression Jamie couldn't interpret. Fear? Anticipation?

She leaned forward and pulled her purse around to her lap. Jamie kept her eyes roaming across all the players in the room, finding the zipper of her purse by touch. She started to pull it open, then stopped.

"I want assurances Trixie and I can depart unharmed and you won't bother us ever again before I hand anything over." Jamie hardened her gaze. "I don't know whose finger was dropped on my doorstep, but it doesn't appear to be my sister's."

Trixie looked down at her hands, gripping the matchbook tightly.

No one moved. No one spoke.

"Maybe I should just see what is so important in this envelope?"

Blue Tie smirked at her. "Go right ahead."

She unzipped her purse and pulled out the envelope. Jamie felt the weight of them watching her, heavy, intense.

She lifted the envelope flap and pulled out a folded sheet. Puzzled by the lack of concern shown by the watchers, she slowly unfolded the paper.

"YOU ARE INVITED TO A SURPRISE PARTY FOR JAMIE HOLDREN!" screamed the headline.

Rapidly, she scanned the next few lines, which listed today's date and time and the location: Humphrey's Oasis Dude Ranch.

Jamie looked up, mouth hanging open, to see Trixie jumping up and down.

"SURPRISE! SURPRISE! I got you! Surprise!"

Both men in suits were grinning broadly, and Cowboy had left her side to open the front door. Her family and friends came streaming in.

"Surprise! Happy birthday!" they chorused. "Trixie had it all live-streaming to the bunk house!" The crowd surrounded her, smiling and chattering.

"Smooth move, spilling that water on yourself," her brother laughed.

Trixie crossed the room and pulled Jamie up into a hug.

"Happy birthday, sis," she whispered in her ear. "Love you."

Jamie pulled back and slugged her in the shoulder. Hard. "Ow!"

"You rat! I was terrified! How could you do this to me?" Jamie reared back to punch her again, but a laughing Red Tie pulled Trixie back and wrapped his arms around her protectively. Trixie leaned into him, smiling, and he dropped a kiss on her head.

"You practically *dared* me on Friday to surprise you for your birthday. So...I did." She stared Jamie down, challenging her to deny the victory.

Jamie looked around the room filled with people excitedly discussing the "kidnapping" and Jamie's water spill. She spotted Cowboy watching her by the front door, a teasing grin on his face. Blushing from head to toe, her lips curved up to answer his smile. Turning back to Trixie, Jamie was flummoxed. She wanted to throttle her. To shake her until her teeth rattled. To hug her, glad she was safe. To thank her for the most unforgettable birthday ever. Finally, she just threw up her hands.

"You got me. You got me good." She shook her head grinning, then grimaced. "Where did you get that creepy finger?"

Trixie unwrapped herself from Red Tie's arms and turned to present him to Jamie.

"This is Todd. He's a sculptor. I met him and Dale," she gestured towards Blue Tie, "Friday, after you left. Dale directs plays at the local theater. I told them about your birthday challenge and the three of us came up with this little drama." Trixie bounced with delight, reliving the victory.

"Todd made a model of my pinky from ceramic and clay, using one of my spare acrylic nails, while Dale contacted his buddy, Colton Humphries, who owns this place. I typed up the instructions and delivered the little package." Trixie held up her hands, fingers splayed. "It was a really good match don't you think?" She twirled around in delight.

Jamie grabbed Trixie's shoulders and gave her an exasperated shake. "Seriously. I was terrified."

Trixie stood still and her smile dropped. Jamie pulled her in close.

"I couldn't bear it if something bad happened to you."

They embraced in a tight hug, then after a moment, Jamie began to deliberately squeeze harder. Trixie gasped and tried to squirm free. Jamie planted her feet and continued to crush her sister.

"Jamie, ow..."

Jamie leaned in and spoke into Trixie's ear.

"You got me. You surprised me and you *scared the shit* out of me," she whispered. After a moment, she released some of the pressure on her sister. "All is forgiven if you properly introduce me to the cowboy standing by the door?"

"Deal," said Trixie. "One Colton Humphrey, coming right up."

With a last crushing squeeze, Jamie freed her. Trixie tucked Jamie's arm under her own, drawing her sister to her side.

"Right this way, birthday girl."

Arm in arm, they strolled across the floor. Cowboy straightened as they approached. A surge of heat flushed through Jamie, and her heart began to beat a little faster. Maybe this was a romance novel after all.

The Do-Over

LAURA JINKINS

Cait stood at the kitchen sink, anxiety causing the muscles in her neck and arms to tense as she gripped the edge of the counter. The storm mocked her through the window—the sky ominous, its dark clouds heavy with rain threatening to crash earthward any second. A sudden bolt of lightning cut a jagged swath across the heavens; the lights flickered and the hair on her arms prickled, shaking her to action. She retrieved two hurricane lamps from the top shelf of the small pantry. Setting them on the counter, she jerked open the junk drawer and rifled through its contents. A lighter or a book of matches had to be there. The lights flickered again, and she looked more urgently.

There.

In the back corner of the drawer, she spied a glint of gold and pulled it from the jumble. A matchbook.

Thunder rumbled across the sky and Cait felt the beach house vibrate ever so slightly. The storm would soon release its full fury, and she didn't want to be caught in the dark.

She quickly lit the two lamps, then stuck the matchbook in her pocket.

Leaving one lamp in the kitchen, she carefully carried the other to the side table by Sam's chair. After wrapping herself in his old navy and orange afghan to ward off the storm's chill, she sank into the worn cushions of the Mission chair. Sitting there, wrapped in his afghan, somehow made her feel closer to him. If only...the rain pounded the roof and she gritted her teeth against the remembrance of a night just like this one, full of stormy rage. The night Sam disappeared. Their fifth anniversary. Six months ago.

The lights flickered again and went out, but the hurricane lamp continued to shine with a warm glow. Thank goodness she'd found the matches. She pulled the book from her pocket and turned it carefully in her fingers. The bold black font against the glimmering gold foil proclaimed *Vargo's*. An elegant matchbook from an elegant restaurant. Earlier she'd been frantic to stave off the darkness, not really cognizant of anything other than making sure she had light. Now she gently opened the book once again and studied the rows of matches. There were six matches missing from the book. She closed the book, holding it in her open palm, tilting it this way and that as the light made the foil gleam. Gleaming just as it had when Sam plucked it from the bowl at the maître d's station at Vargo's years ago.

* * *

"What do you mean you never went to prom?" Sam's eyes were wide with disbelief.

Cait shrugged her shoulders. "I never went to prom. I was busy finishing high school...Mom and Dad were gone." She picked at an imaginary bit of lint on her jeans. "Things were weird. Being an emancipated orphan at sixteen..."

"I know. But I just find it hard to believe no one asked you." He looked at his very adorable girlfriend and shook his head. "I just don't get it."

"Well, did YOU go to prom?" she asked, reaching over and poking his broad chest.

He chuckled wryly. "Kind of."

"What does that mean?"

"Just that. Kind of."

"Spill it."

He shook his head in resignation at her wide hazel eyes. It was so difficult to refuse her when she looked at him like that. "Okay. Let me preface this by saying I was a punk when I was in high school. So, don't judge me, okay?" She nodded.

"I had a surfing buddy back then. His name was Skip. We did just about everything together. He was without wheels and I had a rusty car held together with a lot of Bondo. It was so ugly! Skip wasn't too proud to ride in it when he needed to get somewhere, though." Sam laughed. "Man, that car really was a hunk of junk. But it ran okay, and it would get us to the beach with our boards when the surf was up. Anyway, prom came around and we asked a couple of girls to go. Got the tuxes, got the flowers for the girls. Even persuaded my sister to loan us her much more decent wheels. And then we heard the surf report. The waves were supposed to be ripping that night!"

Cait's eyes grew wider, dismay in her voice as she antici-pated the end of the story. "You DIDN'T!"

He grinned sheepishly. "We did. We stood them up. Grabbed our boards and headed for the beach, and man, the report was spot on! Some of the biggest waves I've ever seen.

I know it was a really crappy thing to do, but MAN! Those were some of the tastiest waves I think I've ever surfed." His grin faded as he saw the dismay shift to disappointment. "I know. I should be...I am ashamed."

"What happened to the girls?"

"Eh. They were mad, of course. Talked smack about us for a few weeks, but we had pretty thick skin. It was always a funny story until now." He picked at his fingernails for a couple of minutes, then abruptly looked up at her. "How about a do-over?"

"What do you mean?"

"Well, I obviously screwed up my high school prom and you never had one. What if we have a do-over?"

"Sam, we're in college! Don't you think that's kind of silly?"

"Not at all. I don't think taking my girl out for a night on the town is silly at all. What do you say? Caitlin O'Keefe, would you do me the honor of attending the prom with me?"

She laughed. "You're an absolute nut, Sam Murphy, but yes. I will go to the prom with you." She paused a second, waggled a finger at him, and continued, "As long as you don't stand me up."

* * *

Sam looked in the mirror, straightening his shoulders and running his hand along his freshly shaved jaw. His blue eyes crinkled at the corners as he smiled, twinkling from under a mop of sun-bleached curly blond hair. He'd planned on going for broke—renting a tux, prom style, but practical Cait talked him out of it. She firmly stated she had no intention of wearing a Scarlett O'Hara ballgown, and he would be just fine in a suit. With a mixture of disappointment and relief, he used their "prom" as an excuse to buy a sharply tailored navy Ralph Lauren suit on sale, complete with crisp white dress shirt and black tie. Classic and professional, it would work well for special occasions and job interviews after he graduated.

Their reservation at Vargo's was for 7:00, but to enjoy the full experience he wanted to be sure they arrived early. He glanced at his watch, grabbed his wallet and keys from the counter and headed toward the door, then did a one-eighty to retrieve the corsage from the fridge. He paused at the door for a moment to make sure he wasn't forgetting anything else and then was on his way.

* * *

She opened the door before he even finished knocking. The expression on his face was full of enthusiastic approval, and she blushed with relief. Even though this evening was a "prom do-over," for both of them, Cait knew it would be frivolous and a little childish to buy a traditional prom dress. She wore a cocktail dress of silvery grey charmeuse that she'd been lucky enough to find at the thrift shop on the square for the reasonable price of $35. The bodice of the sleeveless frock was made of heavily embroidered lace with a high neckline; the skirt fit her curves perfectly, falling just above the knee. She finished off her ensemble with strappy silver heels the thrift shop proprietor had thrown in for five dollars, and a vintage Whiting & Davis mesh bag that had been her mother's. Her auburn hair fell around her shoulders and she'd kept her makeup to a minimum, just as Sam liked it.

"Wow." He just stood there, slack jawed. Then he must have realized how dumb he looked and immediately recovered. "You look amazing..." He held out the clear plastic box holding the corsage. "It's a wrist corsage."

"Thank you." She took the small arrangement of white bud roses from the box and slipped it over her wrist. "It's perfect." She felt herself blushing again, hesitating, and then motioning toward the door. "I guess we should go?"

Sam fumbled reaching for the door, nodding quickly in agreement. "Yes. Definitely. Come on." He stood aside to let her walk through first, stepped back so she could lock the door, and then hurried ahead to his car so he could hold the door open for her. The evening had all the awkward feelings of a high school prom. And then they were on their way.

* * *

The restaurant was nestled in an idyllic woodland setting, the kind of place that catered to people who not only cared about food, but about ambience. After parking the car, Sam helped Cait from the passenger side, commenting more than once on how amazing she looked. The guys in her class had to have been idiots! He took her arm in his and began to walk away from the entrance. She hesitated and said, "Um, Sam? The restaurant is the other way..."

"We have about thirty minutes before our reservation. Let's go check out the park."

They took a leisurely stroll around the grounds along pathways that wound through clusters of pink and white azalea bushes, crossing and then stopping midway on a bridge that spanned a lake. On the opposite bank, a flamboyant peacock spread its tail feathers in an extravagant display of green, turquoise, purple, and deep royal blue. While they stood hand in hand, a pair of swans swam out from under the bridge toward the other side. Cait's face lit up even more, if that was possible.

"Sam! Look!" She pointed at the graceful pair making their way toward a sun dappled spot on the water. They slowed their swim, and stopped face to face, in that way swans will do such that their heads and necks form a heart. He couldn't have planned this more perfectly.

"Did you know that swans mate for life?"

"No...I did not know that." She looked up at him shyly and he smiled broadly.

"Yes, they do." He pulled her toward him, one arm wrapped around her waist, and gently tucked a ringlet of hair behind her ear, then kissed her forehead...the curve of her cheek...and then her lips. Time stood still for a moment, in spite of the increasing tempo of their hearts.

Sam reluctantly pulled away from her and glanced down at his watch. "Oh, look at the time! Our table should be ready about now." He winked at her. "I hear they make a mean fettuccine alfredo."

* * *

From beginning to ending, their "prom" was wonderful. She still remembered the perfectly prepared pasta, the delight of the tableside Cherries Jubilee performance, and dancing under fairy lights strung across the terrace. The highpoint of the evening, however, would always be standing on the bridge watching the two swans swim toward that golden patch of sunlight. Even now, Cait could see them in her mind's eye while she waited out the raging storm in Sam's old chair. She could hear his voice asking...no, telling her the beautiful birds were lifelong partners. As she thought she and Sam would be.

She looked at the matches remaining in the book and felt a wave of despair overtake her. Sam had given her the book on their way out the door that evening. A souvenir. She had told him, "What do I need these for? I don't smoke." He had chuckled and said, "There are all kinds of fires to light, babe. Never know when they might come in handy."

A little less than two months later he had proposed to her and two months after that they'd gotten married. She hadn't really thought about the matchbook again until their first anniversary rolled around. Money was a bit tight and so they'd ordered pizza and bought a cheap bottle of wine. She'd done her best to recreate an intimate Italian bistro: a red checkered tablecloth and an empty wine bottle with a blue candle stuck in it. She lit the candle with the first match from the matchbook, and they celebrated their first year talking about their plans and dreams while the candle wax slowly dripped down the sides of the bottle. The next year money wasn't so tight, but the memory was sweet, so they did it again. The second match for the second candle. Match three for the third year. Match four the year after that. The candle wax increased, different colors intermingling layer after layer, and so did their memories year after year.

Their fifth anniversary seemed like it should accord something new, something special. They were both working now, and Sam suggested they go out for a special dinner. The old wine bottle-cum-candleholder stayed in the cabinet, the matchbook in the junk drawer. They went out to dinner, but things were off...Sam went surfing to decompress, the storm struck, and she never saw him again.

The glow of the hurricane lamp drew her attention and she said, "You should have been match five." She wished they'd ordered pizza and lit another candle in the old wine bottle with the fifth match. Maybe Sam wouldn't have taken his board out. Maybe he would have stayed home. A tearless sob rattled through her body. Rising from the chair, she walked back into the kitchen, opened the junk drawer, and returned the matchbook to the corner from which it came.

She would not use another match from the book.

Not until Sam was there to blow it out.

Duck Hunt
with Dad

A J JINKINS III

In honor of James Lanford and his Pop

Early morning darkness encapsulated the world around me except for the bubble of light cast by the Coleman lantern burning on the open tailgate of the green Ford step-side. Dad reached into the bed of the truck to get our supplies. We had already gotten our shotguns from the rack in the cab's back window; they were safely resting against the flared rear fender. The cold permeated me as I watched the vapor from my exhalations disappear in the wind like the smoke my father blew out from one of his Lucky Strike cigarettes. I resisted the urge to attempt a smoke ring. Rubbing my gloved hands together, bobbing up and down to dispel the chill, I was grateful my old man had advised me to wear two layers of clothes under my camouflage jumpsuit. My full-face mask was riding high upon my head because when I pulled it down over my face, I felt restricted. I sniffled slightly and knew my nose was already red and dripping. Dad glanced toward me and asked, "You alright?" I nodded and smiled, though the truth of it was that I was not completely alright. I was not accustomed to waking up this early and was pretty uncomfortable being out here along the cold humid banks of Holiday Bay at this hour of morning...night. But I was also excited to be on this hunt with my old man. Up until now, he had regarded me as a child needing looking after, but his invitation to go duck hunting with him meant, in my mind, that he might be starting to see me as a man. I had to prove myself to him. In my young, arrogant mind, I was confident I was up to the task.

Dad reached into a metal olive-drab green container and produced two new boxes of Winchester .20-gauge shotgun shells, one of which he pushed toward me and nodded in the direction of the guns. I rushed to the side of the truck, grabbed one in each hand, and gingerly brought them back to where Dad stood, slowly resting them to lean against the edge of the tailgate. Dad nodded his approval and we both turned to sit on the tailgate of the truck. Looking out into the darkness, he reached into his pocket, withdrew a small pack with a red target on it, the familiar label of his smokes, and pulled out one of the unfiltered sticks. After putting the cigarette between his lips, he reached into another pocket and produced a small box of matches with a caricature of a pelican resting on top of a weathered, rope-shrouded piling. We both looked at the matchbox, smiled, and looked at each other as he lit up. The Rusty Pelican had always been one of our family's favorite places to eat. One of those memories that creates a warmth in you at the thought of it. He shook out the match flame, licked the burnt tip, and tossed it into the darkness. Taking a slow drag of the cigarette, Dad leaned back and, peering into the nothingness, began his instructions.

"Okay son. Up to now all you've shot was clay pigeons back on the ranch. This is no different, really. Just remember to stay ahead of the target and you'll do fine. Now, there are twenty shells in a box, so you have plenty of ammo. Just make sure you remember all the safety rules I taught you. You got your earmuffs?"

"Yes sir." I nodded vigorously and smiled to reassure him I was ready.

He placed a box of shells in my hands, surprising me with how heavy twenty shells could be. Dad zipped up his duffel bag and tossed it back into the truck bed, snuffed the flame of the lantern, slammed the gate shut, and turned toward the bay. "C'mon then." I followed close behind in the dark. Better to let him walk into a branch or trip on a root than me.

Now that we were moving closer to the "kill zone," as I called it in my overconfident, young, adrenaline-infused mind, I no longer noticed the chill. Dad and I walked to the edge of the bay where we found a great spot to lay in wait. A few small scrub brushes and several tall trees whose branches still held onto some of their more stubborn leaves provided us a good measure of cover. Dad removed and pocketed the few items left in the bucket he carried: a duck whistle, a knife, his smokes, and a box of matches in a plastic case. He turned the empty bucket over and sat on it. I mimicked him with my own bucket. Once we had loaded our shotguns and were settled in place, he withdrew the duck call from his breast pocket and blew into it twice, then stowed the it away again. I wondered why he was so stingy with the calls. I mused, if two quacks were good, then four would be great! But I dared not disturb the silence and disclose my ignorance. Just assumed he knew what he was doing.

After a while, a reddish line appeared on the horizon, just above the opposite coastline of the bay. The nothingness we had been looking at began to reveal elusive shapes that could be a man, a beast, or a tree root. We sat quietly, watching intently, waiting; the only sound was our breaths slowly being inhaled then exhaled. The reddish line magically transformed into thin gold, widening while the chilly air began to warm up to a survivable degree, and I knew that in moments, the hunt would be on. I felt like a cat, sitting motionless while every muscle in me quivered with the excitement of finally reaching the climax of the hunt. My knee bobbed up and down from restless anticipation, and when Dad looked over at me with "the look," I had to force myself to remain still and silent. We sat, waiting for all them ducks to wake up and start flying over us.

We sat. And we sat. And we sat.

The birds must have been sleeping late because we had not seen even one lousy duck yet, and I was beginning to think that we were wasting our time, freezing in the brush for no reason. I whispered to Dad, "Maybe they wont be flying this early in the season." Dad just quietly shushed me and continued to stare at the horizon. As the sun's light stretched from the horizon and the area around me suddenly appeared, a small, flat stone attracted my attention. After a short mental debate, I gently leaned forward and ever-so-slowly picked up the worn rock, then leaned back. A furtive glance Dad's way indicated that he either hadn't notice my movement or, more likely, chose to ignore it. I turned the smooth stone over and over in my gloved hand

and impulsively threw it toward the water in an attempt to make it skip. Dad turned in exasperation and just glared at me. After a few moments, he reached into his pocket, pulled out his cigarettes and the box of matches with The Rusty Pelican logo printed on it, and lit one up. Sucked the smoke deep into his lungs and let it relax him. Then whispered to me, "Tell you what, son. You might be right. Let's increase our chances by splitting up." He leaned toward me pointing with his gloved hand. "You walk quietly toward that other side of the bay to where that stand of trees is and see if the pickings are any better. I'll stay here just in case. Okay?" *I get to move? By myself?* Naturally, I agreed to this plan. I got up and righted my bucket, putting my box of shells into it, and turned toward the spot he had indicated. Dad and I nodded at each other and I was off.

By the time I reached the trees that Dad had pointed me to, the temperature had risen to a comfortable level and the fauna began to come out and stir. Squirrels darted about looking for food while fish began swimming more actively creating ripples in the calm water. The birds began chirping and the wooded shoreline came to life. I settled down along the shore under a tree and readied myself. Within ten minutes, I heard a noise that sounded like a tree branch falling. The noise must have startled some ducks because they took flight not too far away. I raised my shotgun and followed the fleeing birds. When they were within the same distance as the clay pigeons I was used to shooting, I pulled the trigger once, re-sighted, and pulled again. One bird started flapping its wings wildly and headed for an awkward landing near the shore. I excitedly pulled on my waders and rushed toward the flapping bird. By the time I reached the duck, he was dead. I had my first kill, and I knew Dad would be proud of me.

Now that my initiation was complete, I felt like a professional hunter. I moved further down the shoreline and hunkered down to wait again. Half hour later, another flock of ducks appeared overhead and I got another one. This was getting exciting and I was feeling very accomplished. Later in the morning, after I had spent all twenty shells, I started working my way back to Dad's spot, all the while lugging four dead ducks with me. It was a long haul, but I was so proud I felt I was walking on a cloud. I reached the other site to find Dad gone and the area cleaned up already, so I made my way back to the truck. When Dad saw me approaching, he called out to me, "How'd you do?" I smiled the biggest grin I could and held up my bounty. "I got four! How did you do?" Dad seemed very pleased and helped me relieve myself of the ducks and my gear. He said," I got two."

I danced around, hooted, and hollered in my exuberance. "I shot TWICE as many as you! Woo-hoo! "While I was celebrating, Dad simply watched passively with one of those annoyed grins on his face, shaking his head.

"'Nuff celebrating, son. Time to git. This hunt ain't done"

We unloaded the guns, wiped them down with a rag, and Dad put them back in the gun rack. We righted our buckets, loaded them with our gear and walked them back to the truck as well. Once we were all loaded up, we hopped in the truck for the drive home. All the while, I was chanting, boasting about how I got four to Dad's two. Dad just stared at the road ahead. I could sense he was slightly annoyed, but I didn't care...this was MY time.

Before Dad could even pull the emergency brake of the truck, I had jumped out, grabbed my ducks, and hollered at

Mama to come out and look. Wiping her hands on a dish rag, she saw the four birds I held up and looked at Dad. He smiled and said, "He did good." As I regaled Mama with my experiences, Dad unloaded the gear. He carefully wiped down the guns with a rag and some Schoppe's oil, then placed them in their slots in the gun cabinet and locked them in. Next, he set up the sawhorses with an old door we used as a cleaning station. Together, we cleaned the ducks. He showed me the proper techniques to maximize the meat usage from each bird. After the meat was packaged, labelled, and stored in the freezer, Dad said, "I'll finish cleaning up here. If you'll go fetch the shells out of the truck for me, then you can get yourself cleaned up for lunch."

I ran out to the truck in the driveway, opened the passenger door, and grabbed my empty box off the floorboard. I couldn't reach Dad's box, so I had to go around to the driver's side. I opened the driver's side door, reached in, and grabbed the box. It was heavy. My brow furrowed and I became a bit confused. The box felt full. I pulled it close to me, opened the top, and could not believe what I saw. I stood motionless as I counted nineteen shells still in that box. Dad had shot two birds with one shell. I picked up the box, went back into the garage, set my empty box on the table, then looked him in the eyes as I set his box next to mine. "Good hunt, Dad." He looked into my eyes with that knowing look, grinned, and continued to clean the table. I turned and walked soberly into the house to get a shower with a whole new respect for my dad,

Ethel Vail Elementary, 1958

DIANA RECKART

Maggie rushed into her office as quickly as she could, hopeful that she wouldn't run into anybody. A sigh of relief escaped her lips as she shut the door. Gloria would be arriving soon and she had to make sure she did not see her face to face. After taking a deep breath, she sat down at her desk and tried to organize her work for the day. Instead, she found herself just shuffling papers, unable to focus.

Ring, ring. The sound startled her. Picking it up, she heard Mrs. Davis' voice on the other line.

"Mrs. Jameson? Mrs. Jameson, it's Ruby Davis."

Maggie could hear the years in Ruby's voice. She was the oldest teacher at the school and easy to recognize by the scratchy voice that had been roughened by years of classroom lectures and cigarettes. Because of her tenure, she always made her calls directly to the principal.

"Mrs. Jameson, I woke up in the middle of the night and couldn't get back to sleep. I'm afraid I am just too tired to make it to class today. Can you please call a substitute for me?"

The words stung. She thought about her own night. She had gotten to bed at a decent time but was shaken awake. How long had she slept? It was at least three AM before the terror had stopped.

"Yes, Mrs. Davis, I'll take care of it. We will see you to-morrow," she said, hoping to hide the irritation in her voice. What a blessing if only she too could stay home and catch up on her sleep.

Gloria arrived in the outer office. Maggie could hear her moving about and see her shadow beyond the frosted glass door. Maggie cracked open her door, hiding behind it as she called out to her secretary.

"Gloria, can you get a sub for Mrs. Davis? She called in today."

Gloria answered in the affirmative, turning to look at Maggie, but she had shut the door as quickly as she had opened it. Sitting back down, she picked up the papers again. The semester reports needed to be taken care of, but it was so hard to concentrate. The events of the prior night kept replaying over and over in her head. Her eyes suddenly felt hot and before she could help it, tears were streaming down her face. She grabbed her handkerchief to dab at them only to realize that her face was still swollen.

A knock at the door interrupted her thoughts.

"Mrs. Jameson, it is time for morning announcements," Gloria said as she poked her head into the office.

Maggie kept her back to her. Had that much time passed already?

"OK, Gloria. I will be right out."

The intercom system was in Gloria's office. She had to venture out there to do the announcements. Well, there was no choice to be made; it had to be done. She grabbed her pancake makeup out of her desk drawer and dabbed at her eyes. Looking at her reflection in the compact mirror, she wondered if you could make anything out or if it just looked like a dark shadow. No matter, it was time to run the gauntlet. She opened the door to go into the outer office, keeping her head down and letting her chestnut hair fall over her face. Thank goodness she had resisted the bouffant hairdos so popular now and had kept the flip. It was a useful tool for disguising what she did not want shared.

She rushed over to the microphone that was kept on the sidebar. Gloria slid her the announcement papers. Taking a big gulp of air, her voice sounded stronger than her feelings.

"Good morning boys and girls. Welcome back to class today. We have some special announcements..."

Somehow, she managed to get through them without stumbling. *Focus,* she thought. She had a job to do and it wasn't worrying about herself; it was taking care of these kids. After finishing the last words about the upcoming school carnival, she shut the microphone off and handed the papers back to Gloria. She did not turn to look her in the face. Did Gloria know? Looking at her would either give her secret away or make her realize that it wasn't even a secret. Both would be disasters that she couldn't even begin to face.

As she stepped back into her office, she said, "Please cancel my appointments for today. I have got to get those semester reports reviewed and I will need the extra time. Put them on my calendar for tomorrow."

"Yes, ma'am," Gloria said softly. "I will take care of it."

Maggie wondered if the softness in Gloria's voice meant she knew. Regardless, there was nothing she could do now. She sat down at the desk and tried to work. Making progress on the reports helped distract her mind but images would pop back up and break her concentration. She found herself fiddling with a red, white, and blue matchbook. The cover read "Elect Jackie Scoff for Sheriff." The fifth-grade teacher, Mr. Johnson, must have left it the other day when they had discussed the class field trip. He always ended up lighting up a cigarette whenever he came to her office, much to her dismay. The book had been sitting on the corner of her desk and for some reason she found solace in flipping the cover with her thumb. The repetitive motion soothed her when thoughts of last night, and the many other nights, poked at her. As she laid the book down with the saddle facing her, she noticed the big, bold red letters proclaiming "TIME FOR A CHANGE."

Knock, knock.

Maggie turned to the door but kept her face down, allowing her hair to fall slightly over it. "Yes."

It was Gloria again. She cracked the door open and leaned in.

"Mrs. Jameson? Miss Andrews has sent a student down to visit you. I told her you were tied up today but she said it was important for you to deal with the student."

"OK, Gloria. Send the student in."

In the few moments she had before the child entered the office, she turned her back and quickly grabbed her compact to once again freshen the makeup on her face. The quiet plodding of feet and click of the door shutting signaled the student's entrance. She turned around, keeping her head down until she was facing the door. She looked up from beneath the brown bangs that fell across her face.

A young boy stood before her. His own head down, eyes glued to the floor.

"Well, young man," her voice of authority speaking. "What seems to be the problem?"

Shuffling his feet, a small voice spoke, "I didn't have my homework." Gloria was grateful that he had not raised his head to look at her. Perhaps she could keep her secret.

"That is hardly a reason to be sent to the principal's office. Is there more that you need to tell me? I am pretty sure Miss Andrews had a better reason to send you."

After wiping his eyes with the back of his hand, he shakily added, "Well, ma'am, I haven't turned it in all week. She gave me this note to give to you."

He walked up to the desk and laid the note down, then quickly retreated away from the desk. Maggie grabbed the note without looking at him. Miss Andrews had sealed it with tape. Breaking it open, she read:

John has not turned in his homework for a week. Please discuss it with him. I have a feeling there is another issue.

Miss Andrews

"Well, John, why aren't you doing your work?" Maggie had to look directly at him now so she could see his reaction. He still kept his eyes fixed on the floor, the blonde hair on top of his head hanging towards the ground, obscuring his face.

"Ma'am, I *have* done my homework. It just wasn't good enough to turn in." He had one foot on top of the other now, pressing his toe down hard on the grounded foot.

Maggie was used to excuses. This little man wasn't about to get away with this one.

"Really? And who is to say it is not good enough? Shouldn't your teacher decide that *after* you turn it in?"

John still did not look up. He clasped his hands together, squeezing them so hard his knuckles were white.

"I was told, it wasn't good enough to give to my teacher." His voice was barely a whisper as he strained to say them.

Maggie craned her neck to hear him and finally in frustration said, "John, that is ridiculous. Who would say such a thing to you?"

"My dad!" he said tearfully, raising his face briefly with the exclamation. He quickly covered his face with his hands and turned his head back down. But it was enough, enough of a glimpse for Maggie to see what the problem was. For when he lifted his tender, innocent face to her, she could see the big purple bruise that crossed his cheek. She could see the puffy eyes that still blazed red. She could see as if she was looking in a mirror.

The gasp she let out wasn't intentional. It was her reaction to the palette in front of her. Silence captured her voice as her thoughts raced in so many directions. Focusing her senses, she softened her tone and said, "It looks like we need to do something, don't we?"

"Ma'am, I don't know what you can do. Nobody does anything."

Maggie sat there for a moment. This little boy needed help. She needed ...

She got up and walked around her desk. Kneeling down in front of John, she lifted his head. He cautiously looked at her face and quickly gulped in some air at what he saw.

"Well, John," she said, ignoring his initial reaction. "I promise you this. *I* am going to do something."

He looked at her quizzically but then breathed a sigh of relief.

"You go back to class. Don't worry about your homework for this week. I will talk with Miss Andrews about that."

A glimmer of hope crossed his face. He turned to the door, but he paused after opening it.

"You'll keep your promise?"

"Absolutely! And if you ever need to come to the principal's office again, you don't need to wait for Miss Andrews to send you. Feel free to come any time."

A shy smile graced his face and, just like, that he was gone.

She stayed there for a few moments, staring at the spot where he had once stood.

Time for a change, she reminded herself. For him and for...

Walking to the door, she opened it wide, "Gloria, "she declared. "Bring me the phone book."

S3 Walkers

LYNNETTE BROOKS

Summer in Texas can make a morning walk. Literally. The sunlight marches quickly across the neighborhood, changing shapes and moving shadows, highlighting hidden gems. It also scorches everything and everyone in its path as the day progresses, including us short furry folks if we get a late start.

I have been told I am a handsome fellow with a good disposition, even at my advanced age. And I don't mind telling you that I consider myself quite a ladies' man. Girls of all kinds are attracted to me. My name is Happy. Chica, my roommate, is a lovely bi-colored lady with just a hint of hoity-toity about her. We both like to walk. Fortunately, our mistress, Lynnette, shares our delight in the doings around our neighborhood.

Every walk has the potential to become a grand adventure. Today is no exception. Mornings are the best time, according to our mistress. She says hot sidewalks can blister foot pads. Not sure what a blister is, but it sounds bad. Lynnette calls this exercise, but for Chica and me, it is all about the fascinating olfactory stimulation. Today is trash day. Excessive heat and light can, and will, raise the scent of whatever refuse is inside the bags. However, it quickly destroys most smells from the outside of the trash bags, in the grass, and on our favorite signposts. We know. We are experts.

Trash days, are our favorite days to walk. Lynnette indulges us when the weather is good. If it is raining or the sidewalks are wet, Chica stays home. She is such a girly girl.

Personally, I find it difficult to contain my excitement when Lynnette pulls out my blue harness and matching leash, regardless of the weather. Chica likes to play coy. She pretends to be afraid or wants Lynnette to chase her. These actions are unbecoming and certainly beneath me. And they waste precious time we could use to explore. Chica and I like to sniff every bag we encounter. If we are lucky, the bag handler will not have washed his or her hands recently and left some really good smells so we can compare notes on what we find. We look for information on what the neighbors have eaten, which person took the trash out, and if another dog passed this way earlier, or a cat. Personally, I like it when a cat rubs a bag. Cats like to say hi without being obvious, unless it is one of the local toms. They are rather pushy. We also like to know if anyone has had visitors since we last came by. You would be surprised what we can figure out by sniffing the outside of a trash bag. The holidays are the best, all that wrapping paper, cookie crumbs, homemade rolls, and ham, oh my goodness. Yes indeed, the holidays make trash days extra special.

Our mistress never rushes us on these walks. She calls them "strolls" for some reason unknown to me. I have heard her tell our Johnny that we never miss an opportunity to sniff an upright object. This statement, although made frequently, never fails to garner a laugh from both humans. They have given us a "team" name: "Stroll, Stop, Sniff" or "S cubed." Compliment or not? Who cares! As long as I get to wear my blue harness and walk the neighborhood, I am delighted.

Chica and I always find exciting things when we go out together. But last week it was Lynnette's turn. She found an oddly shaped matchbook on the sidewalk, that was crawling with ants. Neither Chica nor I could figure out what was so interesting. Normally, Lynnette expresses her ire in a rather colorful verbal manner when trash litters the neighborhood.

This time, Lynnette stopped. She only ever stops when we do, or to visit with a neighbor, so this was out of character for her. She watched as ants walked in lacy swirls on the open face of the matchbook. She appeared to be mesmerized. This fascination confused both Chica and me: Lynnette does not smoke, and Johnny uses a lighter. The few matchbooks to which I have paid attention are square and fold over. Chica noted that matchbooks typically have little sticks inside with a sharp and acrid smell that burns the nose. This remnant was flat, half on the grass, and had an hourglass shape. Chica and I did our thing; sniffing it side to side, front to back, and found nothing to hold our interest. Not much scent at all. It had not been handled by anyone for quite a while.

As Lynnette stood there, gazing at this book, she started talking to herself about drawing, backroads, poetry, and something called Zentangle. Chica and I looked at each other in wonder. This was not normal behavior. Chica asked me, using her quiet voice, if this had ever happened before. I had to admit that it had not, at least not while Lynnette was under my care. After picking the matchbook up, Lynnette got even more excited when she turned it over and saw the wording about a restaurant in Michigan, something with a veggie buffet? After more murmuring, she dropped the empty matchbook in the bag attached to my leash and we started moving again. Weird. Humans are weird sometimes. Ours are always sweet and indulgent. Chica and I talked and decided that adding the word weird to their description, as of this day, had to be done.

As we continued walking, Lynnette kept talking to herself about the book. She started speculating about its journey, the how and why of it. She even mentioned that Michigan is a long way away: no hope of getting there during one of our walks. The artwork advertised a restaurant that was a step up from the Holiday Inns in which we have stayed during some of our past travels, because it made mention of a veggie buffet. Chica and I understand the interest in a buffet.

Regional foods are always interesting when we are allowed to sample bits and pieces. We like travel for new adventures, and as we have learned, the scenery and greenery are always different. And there are always people who want to scratch our ears. Especially women. You see, I think I told you already that I fancy myself a bit of a lady magnet. I have this little dance I do for attention. I wag my tail and lift my ears so the trimmed silky blonde hair blows. It gets them every time. This dance proves I am harmless, and people often approach before asking permission. Lynnette and Johnny are very protective, so this usually means my leash will get shortened while they talk to the new person. I have noticed that little kids are more likely to approach us before adults, but eventually we get them all, no matter where we find them. Ladies of all ages like me, a lot.

I can easily get lost in all the memories of nice people and food we have found in our travels. I talked to Chica about her memories of food and people. She said that her hands-down favorite are family gatherings; as much as it pains me to agree with her, on this I must. With all the little people, food preparation, and genuine chaos, bits of tasty things get dropped. If we are quick, we can do the clean-up. We are, after all, willing to do our part.

Once, on our way to a north Texas camping spot, Johnny and Lynnette stopped at what they described as "a hole in the wall" fish joint. I was almost beside myself by the time they returned to our RV, the scent of fish, fries, hush-puppies, and sweets were making me drool. Lynnette and Johnny were laughing about their hair and clothes smelling like grease. Sometimes a sensitive nose is not a good thing. In my opinion, the best treat they brought us was fresh cooked fries. Greasy, crispy and oh so soft in the middle. We had crab once in Matagorda, that was just ok. But campers at RV Parks where there are a lot of families with little kids are the best; kids will usually let us lick their faces. A perfect way to get a treat if I do say so myself. Chica says that is gross. I did mention her tendency toward la-di-da, right? There is a truck stop about half-way to our grandparents that is always busy. A lot of people stop there to rest, refresh themselves and stretch their legs. Occasionally, a chicken leg or partial sandwich can be found on the ground close to the picnic tables. To get those treats, Chica and I have learned to be fast because we are not "trash eating dogs" according to Lynnette and our Johnny.

All four of us are very fond of veggies; green beans, carrots, and sweet potatoes are personal favorites. A veggie buffet would be a huge plus. Veggies are great treats and low calorie too, so we can keep our svelte physiques. Still, Lynnette kept wondering about the previous owner, or owners, of the lost artifact, asking how it got to Texas, who dropped it and the like. Honestly, I have no idea.

Lynnette's fascination continued as we walked, and she never stopped making up stories for the matchbook and speculating about what stories it could tell if it could talk. As if. Even *I* know a book does not talk, unless it comes from Audible.

Hopefully soon, Lynnette will learn to speak Poodle or Chihuahua. When she does, one of us can tell her Michigan would be an ok destination if we can visit the buffet, and stop, stroll and sniff the sidewalks on trash days.

The Illness Next
Door

CORINNA SEE

Peach St. Clair slid one manicured fingertip between the kitchen window blinds and peeked outside.

The sun glinting off a white Escalade nearly blinded her, so she quickly let the wide wood slat fall back into place, blinking the glare from her green eyes. The neighbors' SUV was in the driveway, which was usually vacant this early in the day. Perhaps they'd recently arrived home. Had they driven their twins to school? Or driven to the local clinic?

Peach poked at the blinds again. Sun spots still clouded her vision; she misjudged the distance and poked too hard, and the blinds clattered against the window. She uttered a small noise of frustration, reached to steady them, and frowned in distaste at a chip in her red nail lacquer.

How long had that been there?

How long *had* it been since she'd had her nails done? Not quite three weeks now since the spa was declared "non-essential" and forced to close.

She brought her thumbnail level with her gaze and knit twin brows: the nail bed was beginning to peek out from under the polish.

Oh, no. That wouldn't do.

She flicked another glance out the window, and then flicked the curtain closed over the slats. Perhaps there would be some sign of the Epleys later...after she figured out what to do about her manicure. She curled her fingers into her palms to hide the unsightly imperfection.

Peach picked up her phone from the kitchen table and straightened the placemat beneath it before consulting the app that compiled her notes. It was early afternoon—if all went as scheduled, Mr. Stanley in the house on the other side should be stepping out to gather his mail right about...

She moved to that window and looked through the blinds. Sure enough, after several seconds, the front door opened and Mr. Stanley shuffled outside in his cardigan and house slippers. As usual, one gnarled hand clutched the carved ebony wood cane she and Lance had given him during their neighborhood's white elephant holiday gift exchange.

Even though white elephant gifts were meant to be entertaining, the term had roots in giving impractical gifts of extravagance, and Peach preferred to take the road of "extravagant practicality" in her gift giving. The Patels, four doors down, had gifted the St. Clairs one of those scrubby dish sponge holders for the kitchen: a clown's head with a wide, open mouth. Peach had hated it immediately, but her husband thought it was hilarious and refused to let her get rid of it. Peach had taken to pushing it out of sight behind a cookbook stand; Lance had taken to pulling it back out, and doing the dishes so Peach wouldn't "accidentally" knock it into the sink to shatter.

Her fingers tapped out a quick notation in her phone, and she placed it back down on the table. All seemed well with Mr. Stanley at least, and in another hour or two, she anticipated noting that he would be watering his prized petunias.

She turned away from her vantage point to survey the kitchen with a critical eye. The stainless-steel hardware and granite countertops were spotless, not a stray crumb or coffee ground in sight. A pressed dish towel, decorated with a spray of embroidered tulips, hung neatly from the oven door handle.

Peach frowned again. Late spring was already giving way to summer; the tulips would need to be replaced with the sunflowers before the week was out.

A large bottle of hand sanitizer encased in an ornamental soap bottle holder stood at attention in the middle of the island, and Peach pumped some into her hand. Knowing the alcohol would dry out her skin, she followed it with a small pump of moisturizer from the bottle on the window-sill above the sink.

She was mulling over the gleaming hardwood floor—*Was that a scuff mark?*—when the back door opened, and she turned abruptly, startled by the sound.

"Hey babe!" Lance shut the door behind him hard enough to make the wood blinds swing and clatter against the glass, as he usually did. He never seemed to notice how it irked his wife.

He greeted her with a kiss on the cheek and a squeeze of her waist before moving past her to get a glass of water.

"Did you finish with the flowerbeds?" She rested her hip against the island, glancing toward the window again.

"I did." Lance drank deeply from the crystal tumbler he had pulled from the cabinet. "Whew, it's a scorcher out there today!"

With his free hand he pulled the dish towel and mopped his forehead; Peach flared her nostrils and turned away so she wouldn't have to see him carelessly toss it on the clean counter.

It's fine. She had planned to toss it into the wash with the rest of the linens anyway.

"Did you see anything of the Epleys?" she inquired.

"No—" His reply was interrupted by several rough coughs. Peach took an automatic step back.

When his hacking subsided, he wiped his mouth and re-filled his glass.

"Sorry," he said. "Water must've gone down wrong."

He drank again, coughed, and set the tumbler in the sink. "No sign of the neighbors. Why?"

Peach shrugged. "I was just wondering. It's been several days, hasn't it?"

"Guess so. Might be quarantining."

Peach tensed and her green eyes flicked toward her iPhone.

"Perhaps we should call—"

She didn't have time to finish before Lance sighed deeply. "Oh, no, Peach—not this again."

"If they have the virus, the Health Department needs to know about it!"

"It's not our job to inform them!" he argued.

"But—"

"No." He shook his head. "No way. Look, if you're so worried, why don't you just call the neighbors to check on them?"

"Well, if they're infected, they're certainly not going to *admit* it!"

"Just call them and see if they're home then, and if they are sick, then you can rest assured that they're not out spreading it around. And if they're not sick, no harm done. Right?"

Not right, but she saw no point in trying to explain that to him.

Peach's hand twitched toward the phone, and Lance moved around the island as if to block her.

"If you call 911 for this crap again, eventually they're not going to come when there's a *real emergency*." He leveled a glare at her even as his shoulders slumped with fatigue, tired of rehashing the subject, and she felt her defenses flare.

"You're not honestly still mad that—"

"—that you called 911 because you thought *I* was infected!?" Lance scoffed. "Nope. I'm not still mad."

His statement dripped with a sarcasm that did not escape her, and he wouldn't meet her eyes. For an instant, she felt guilty, and tried to temper her husband's ire.

"Well," she said meekly, "at least your test came back negative. That's good news, right? So we know we're safe. But the neighbors—"

"Peach, it's not our job to police our neighbors' health— or the state of their flowerbeds or what color they paint their front door."

She bit down on the inside of her cheek and turned away from him.

Fine.

Peach folded her arms over her blouse and slid the diamond pendant Lance had gifted her for their sixth anniversary back and forth on its delicate chain.

Maybe there wasn't anything for her to worry about. Maybe the Epleys *were* home, which would explain why their car was in the driveway. Maybe they were entertaining friends, which would mean they weren't quarantining and could explain why there was no sign of anybody outdoors—come to think of it, hadn't she seen another car pulling into their driveway not long before?

She craned her neck to peek out the window again but could not discern whether another vehicle might be hiding behind the SUV.

But if they *were* entertaining, they shouldn't be doing that, either, and the authorities should be aware of any breach in the law.

She reached toward her phone again.

"Do we have any decongestants?" Lance opened the cabinet above the coffee bar and rummaged through the medicine bottles as Peach snapped her hand back. "I think my allergies are acting up again. Must've inhaled some pollen while I was weeding."

She supposed she could always look into it later.

"Yes, there should be some." Peach removed the top from the citrus candle on the island and pulled open the junk drawer to search for a matchbook. There were usually several; she pulled out two and flipped open the golden one embossed with a cursive letter *D*—no matches.

"D" for "drat." She sighed.

"Lance, I've asked you not to return spent matchbooks to the drawer." She paused. "Honey."

She hoped that tacking on the endearment would make her sound less annoyed.

"Sorry." He tossed back two caplets, swallowing dry and wincing as they went down. "Agh. That hurt."

"Use water next time." Peach placed the toe of her high heel on the pedal to open the trash can and delicately stepped down; with a flick of her thin wrist, she tossed the empty matchbook inside. She picked up the white one with "Callaway Gardens" printed across the front in green and opened it—success.

Striking a match, she touched it to the trimmed wick until it danced with a lick of flame. After a moment the delightful scent of lemon cookies wafted through the kitchen, and Peach breathed in the aroma, while Lance watched with a *V* of puzzlement puckering his forehead.

"What?" she asked.

"What's the point of buying a candle without any scent? Seems like a waste of money to me."

"I can smell it," she said. "I guess it must be your allergies."

He shrugged. "Must be."

Lance pulled a teacup from a cabinet and a box of tea bags from a drawer. "Do we have any honey? Those pills must have scraped down my throat—it still hurts."

"Yes, yes, it's in the—you know what, just go sit down, and I'll bring you some tea." Peach shooed him out of her kitchen.

"I'm gonna turn the air down, sweetheart," Lance called over his shoulder. "It's warm in here."

"Yes, yes, fine," she murmured, not really listening.

Peach selected a saucer for his teacup, enjoying the delicate *clink* of the china against her clean countertop, and put the teakettle on the stove. While she waited for it to whistle, she used a sanitary wipe on the cabinet, drawer handles and the doorknob, then wiped down the countertop again. After tossing the wipe into the trash, she pumped some hand sanitizer and moved to the window to peek outside again.

Nothing appeared to have changed except the flowerbeds; Lance had done an excellent job of pruning. *But...*

Staring at the flowers, Peach crinkled her eyebrows.

In all the years they'd been together, Lance had never expressed any allergy to pollen.

She picked up her phone and swiped through it quickly, pulling up the note that meticulously detailed their medical histories. Scrolling through, Peach gave a cursory glance to her list of Lance's allergies: penicillin and strawberries; no mention of pollen.

Peach lowered the phone in her hands and chewed on the inside of her cheek in attempt to ignore the anxiety that knotted in her stomach.

What if—?

Just as quickly, she shook the thought away.

"That's not possible," she said, as though, by saying it out loud, it was more likely to be true.

Automatically, Peach reached for the hand sanitizer on the island and rubbed another pump into her hands. She'd been doing everything right—sanitizing, washing, avoiding other people. She was *vigilant* about doing everything right.

But what if Lance—?

No. No! She shook her head again but shifted her gaze to the phone on the table.

Peach took one step in that direction and gripped the edge of the island to prevent herself from going further.

"No ma'am," she chided herself. "You're not doing that again."

She forced her attention away from the table and busied herself pulling a plate from the cabinet and bread from the pantry. She retrieved meat, cheese and condiments from the refrigerator and set about making her husband a sandwich, fixing her eyes on her work.

"Here you go, honey," she said, marching it into the living room as soon as she finished. "How are you feeling?"

"Tired," he said, taking the plate from her and setting it on the table next to his chair.

"Your tea's not ready yet, but I'll get you another glass of water," she chattered, trying to keep herself distracted.

It wasn't really working.

In the kitchen she put everything away, making sure all the jars and bottles in the fridge had the label facing outward. She swept up the bread crumbs and wiped down the countertop, and ran a clean tumbler under the tap.

"Did you put anything on this sandwich, Peach? It doesn't taste like anything."

Peach's vision tunneled. Her chest fluttered; she drew in short, shallow breaths without smelling the scented candle. Her hand shook and water overfilled the glass, spilling over the sides and into the sink.

The teakettle began to whistle.

Fried Clams and Ice Cream

LAURA JINKINS

Daddy had been gone over a month this time, and we were beyond ready for him to come home. Just a few more hours before we'd head to the airport to pick him up from his most recent project; we could hardly wait. His new job working with the engineering group in Friendswood required a lot of travel. Usually he would come home on the weekends, like he did when he oversaw the reconstruction of a turkey processing plant in Louisiana. The first weekend he came home from that particular project, he kept taking deep breaths, exhaling slowly. Mama asked him, "Jimmy, are you okay?" He looked puzzled for a moment and then laughed.

"Do you know how 'foul' a turkey processing plant smells after burning to the ground?" He chuckled at his own joke, very pleased with himself. "I keep trying to get the smell of burned feathers out of my nose." Mama wrinkled her own nose at the thought of the stench and lit a candle.

Another job had him working in Bay City during the week, but again he came home on the weekends. We got used to the rhythm of Daddy leaving for work late Sunday nights and returning home Friday evenings. Mama would hold down the fort. We would go to school, come home, and do our homework. We did okay, but we sure missed our daddy.

He was working out of town one week when the engineering group got a call from Indiana. It was the owner of an oil refinery in Fort Wayne, and there had been an explosion. No one was seriously injured, but the refinery was completely inoperable because the damage was so massive. With a large government contract hanging in the balance, the man said he needed someone *now* who could get the refinery up and running safely as soon as possible. The other men in the engineering group agreed that Daddy had the most knowledge and experience for a reconstruction project of this kind and size, so they sent someone else to finish up the project he was working on. Within twenty-four hours, he was on a plane to Fort Wayne to see what he could do.

Mr. Gladstone's family had started the refinery in the 1940s, back when it was a small fuel stop—hardly even a blip on the map. Over the years, they'd built it into one of the largest fuel refineries in the United States. When he got the call in the early morning hours that there'd been an explosion, his first concern was to make sure all his employees were okay. His second was to get the refinery back up and running because his employees depended on a steady paycheck to provide for their families. The government contract would be canceled if they weren't able to produce the fuel promised, and that meant lay-offs or even the complete shuttering of the refinery. So when one of Mr. Gladstone's assistants picked Daddy up at the airport, he took him straight to the job site—the motor lodge could wait.

The destruction Daddy saw when he and his driver arrived was almost unfathomable. A thick smoke, heavy with a chemical smell, hung in the air from the fires that had been extinguished by the first responders. The refinery workers slowly walked around twisted metal pipes and beams lying this way and that, lost without purpose. Standing alone in the middle of the industrial detritus, Mr. Gladstone looked beaten.

"Hi, there!" Daddy stuck his hand out and Mr. Gladstone accepted the handshake. "I'm Jim Swan. Looks like we've got a lot of work to do." Mr. Gladstone nodded.

"Jim, we do. And we don't have much time to do it. A lot of livelihoods depend on this refinery running, and the longer it's shut down, the further behind we all get on our obligations." He motioned for Daddy to follow him. "Let's go back to my office where we can think clearly without all this smoke fogging our brains."

* * *

A twenty-minute drive carried them to the business district. Mr. Gladstone had offices on the ninth floor of a ten-story building across from City Hall. During the drive, he asked Daddy how his flight had been, where in Texas he lived, was he married...kids? Oh, two? Mr. Gladstone had five of his own, plus a few stepchildren. The pleasantries, the idle chitchat were a thin veil for the tension evident in the tightness of the oilman's jaw. He didn't mention the reason Daddy had flown to Indiana with less than twelve hours' notice until they were both comfortably seated across from each other in his office, a coffee tray on the low table between them. Mr. Gladstone motioned toward two black and gold thermal mugs, steam rising from each. "Help yourself, Jim."

"Don't mind if I do," Daddy said gratefully. He added a couple of spoons of sugar to one of the mugs, as well as a scoop of creamer, and stirred the brew.

"I appreciate your flying up here on such short notice. As you can see, we're in bad shape. I've already talked to two other reconstruction companies. One said it would take a year, the other said six months. Frankly, our employees can't wait that long to get back to work, and by the time we're up and running again, they will all have either gotten new jobs or moved away." Mr. Gladstone let out a heavy sigh, his shoulders dropping slightly, and then took a sip from his mug. "What can you do for us, Jim?"

Daddy weighed his words carefully, slowly stirring the contents of his mug. It was a habit of his—turning the spoon around and around as he pondered the solution to some problem. Fortunately, he had yet to stir a hole through the bottom of his cups. He'd been absorbing the full weight of the refinery's condition from the moment he arrived. He knew this was probably the biggest project he'd tackled yet —if he got the engineering group the job. If they completed the reconstruction successfully, they couldn't begin to put a price on the word of mouth advertising they'd receive. But it stood to reason, if they weren't successful, didn't finish on time, it could damage their standing in the industry for years to come.

"Let me ask you a couple of questions," Daddy started. Mr. Gladstone nodded his assent. "You've got a lot of men standing around without anything to do right now, right? Men that want to be working, want to be earning their paychecks. You've got operators, instrumentation specialists, truck drivers, etc. Let me put them to work on the reconstruction. The more hands we have on deck, the faster this will go."

"I don't have a problem with that at all. I've got about a hundred men who are itching to work." He leaned forward, elbows on knees, hands clasping and unclasping nervously. He looked Daddy in the eye, his face painfully earnest. "Most of these men are second generation Gladstone men. Their fathers worked for my father, and now they work for me. I suppose we all feel a duty to one another to make Gladstone survive and thrive."

Daddy nodded. "If you can have them work around-the-clock shifts, and I can bring two of my associates up here, we can get you operational in thirty days."

Mr. Gladstone's jaw dropped. "Come on. You're pulling my leg, right?"

"No."

"The other companies said at the minimum six months, and you're telling me we can be producing fuel in *one month*?"

"That's exactly what I'm telling you. Provided you hire my group and we can run three eight-hour shifts around the clock. I have all my materials contacts and will start ordering what we need today. As soon as those materials arrive —between twenty-four and thirty-six hours—we'll start reconstruction. Right now, while we're waiting for those materials to come in, we need to get these guys on cleanup. Agreed?" Setting his mug on the tray, Daddy extended his hand confidently as he stood up.

Mr. Gladstone stood as well, grabbing his hand and shaking it vigorously. "I should probably ask how much this is all going to cost, but I don't care. My daddy built this refinery from the ground up, and I have to keep her alive. She's his legacy."

Daddy smiled. "I think you'll find our rates are very reasonable. Thanks for the job."

* * *

For the next four weeks, Daddy worked long, long hours getting the refinery back on its feet. If he wasn't at the plant supervising the crews, he was in an empty conference room pouring over blueprints, making adjustments to the drawings to ensure the refinery was not only up and running by the deadline, but up and running safely. Sometimes he would pack it all up and take it back to his room at the Howard Johnson's Motor Lodge to work. It was only in the privacy of his room that he inwardly acknowledged doubts whether they would make the deadline. He would then attack the plans spread out across the desk with renewed vigor. Checking and double-checking the details. Making sure there was no room in them for the devil.

He'd almost made it to his room when he realized he hadn't eaten since breakfast, and it was nearly 9:00 pm. He made his way back through the lobby to the restaurant to grab a bite to eat. The hostess, a thick, middle-aged woman named Pat, still wore her salt and pepper hair in a bouffant style from fifteen years ago. Even at this late hour, her uniform was crisply pressed, and she looked like she'd just arrived for work. "Hey, Jimmy. You still with us?" Her northeast Indiana accent had the slightest hint of a drawl, which made him even more homesick for Texas.

"A few more days, Pat. Just a few more days." He reached into the jar on the hostess stand and grabbed a book of matches for his end of the day smoke. The orange and turquoise matchbook proclaimed Howard Johnson's as "The Flavor of America," and he had to admit, patting his midsection, the restaurant food had been pretty good. "Is it too late to get some of those fried clams I had the other night? They sure are good."

Pat grinned as she led him to a booth alongside the stretch of windows facing the highway. "I think we still have some. Amy will be taking care of you, and I'm sure she can find out. What would you like to drink?"

He asked for water and a cup of coffee, and Pat went to get his beverages before returning to her hostess stand. It was only a few short minutes before Amy came to take his order. He was happy to learn that it wasn't too late to order those fried clams. They were just so good—thin strips of crunchy goodness, sweet and salty all at the same time, with a quick dip in the tangy cocktail sauce he preferred over tartar, every day of the week and twice on Sunday. The only thing that could improve the meal would be to have his family with him.

"Hey, Amy," he called when she walked near his table again. "Do you know if there's a Howard Johnson's in Houston?"

"Um...I think so, but let me go ask Pat. She's been working here almost as long as HoJo's been around."

"Thanks." He returned his attention to the clams and coleslaw, glancing up briefly to see Pat headed his way.

"There sure is, honey. You trying to find you a HoJo's when you get home, since you're going to miss all of us so much?" She grinned.

"These clams," he began, waving a cocktail sauce anointed clam strip in the air, "are so good. And then there's the ice cream. It's not Blue Bell, but..." Pat's expression shifted from amused to puzzled.

"Blue Bell?"

Daddy laughed. "It's a brand back home. Texans love it. Think it's the best in the country. But seriously, I want to take my family to HoJo's for fried clams and ice cream sundaes—might go straight there from the airport!" His broad smile grew small and he cleared his throat. "God, I miss them."

"I know you do," she said, nodding. She patted his shoulder. "As hard as you and your men have been working, it can't be too much longer, can it?"

"Should be wrapping it up in about six days. I'd be lying if I didn't admit there were a few times I wondered if we'd make it. But it looks like we're going to get it done. I'm real proud of how hard everyone has worked to make the deadline."

"I bet you are," she smiled. "I need to get back to my station now, so I'll let you finish your clams. Do you need anything else?"

Daddy grinned, patted his midsection again and said, "How about a bowl of that butter pecan before I call it a night?"

* * *

A week later, the job was finished, and Mr. Gladstone's refinery was back up and running. He was completely amazed that the reconstruction had come in on time and on budget, with no safety violations or injuries. Daddy met with him at the refinery for one last walkthrough before his assistant took him to the airport.

"Jim, I can hardly believe it. I mean, obviously I must have, because I hired you. When I think back where we were thirty days ago—it just doesn't seem possible, even though I'm seeing it with my own eyes."

"Truth be told, Mr. Gladstone, just between you and me, I'm a little surprised myself." Daddy laughed, and then extended his hand to shake Mr. Gladstone's. "Thank you for the opportunity, sir. It's been tough, but it's been a pleasure."

* * *

A few hours and one airplane change later, Daddy was back home in Texas. We picked him up at Hobby Airport and were so excited to see him! He hugged us all really tight and then it was off to baggage claim for his suitcase. On the way, Daddy asked if we were hungry. It was getting pretty close to dinnertime. Mama looked at us and we nodded. Yes, we could all eat.

"How do y'all feel about fried clams and ice cream?"

Mi-Rai

LYNNETTE BROOKS

On the road again.
Destination chosen.
House sold. Jobs calling.
Together, we go forward.

Car packed. Filled side-to-side.
Bags and food for five.
Dog and toys too.
We need to get moving.

In the driveway, we begin.
Headlights illuminate all we are leaving.
Backing out, swinging 'round.
Darkness covers the land.

Asphalt's glow leads the way.
We are moving; a new home awaits.
Our focus lingers on what we are losing:
Friends, safety, and familiar places.

This trip is to be an adventure.
New places to see along the way.
Parks, rivers, and bridges too.
Traveling west, we follow the sun.

All along Lake Erie's shore,
Games are played.
Questions asked.
Scenery changes.

To pass the time, the children whine:
Are we there yet?
Soon we must escape this car.
It has become small and close.

Seeking sustenance and diversion.
We begin to anticipate a location.
Where we eat must be interesting:
Location, style, color, or façade.

What catches our attention?
Trees of Chinese characters!
Now we know, we will be fine.
Comfort food is on the horizon.

Our hostess greets us at the door.
Wearing skillfully embroidered dark, red silk.
Surrounded by fragrant steam, she leads us to a table.
All distress and whining ceases. Five of us at peace.

Menus in hand, we choose our favorites.
Laughter and chatter flow from within us.
Here we are: weary and wary of what will be.
No matter. Love surrounds us.

Healing will cover our move's sad beginning.
We cannot know what will be.
Together, we will follow the sun.

Faye

CORINNA SEE

Ostensibly it was a candle shop, with a name like Wicks 'N' Sticks. But in addition to candles, the tiny space sold an odd assortment of odds and ends, so that after some months Kristin believed that "Wicks 'N' Sticks" was just another name for odds and ends, bits and pieces, trash and treasures.

Though the shop was always low on trash, because Mr. Yiplow didn't like to lock up without first having emptied the rattan wastebaskets. During the day he kept the shop as spotless as his 78-year-old arthritic hands would allow—considerably more than Kristin would've expected or bothered to manage herself at the ripe old age of 19. While Mr. Yiplow spent time fussing and fretting, Kristin spent most of her time gazing inattentively out the window.

It was a slow day; Thursdays always were. Kristin usually filled her time by arranging the shelves of candles in new ways: grouped by seasonal scents, lined up according to color, or sorted by how interesting she found their names.

"For When You Really Need to Light Something on Fire" was her favorite.

In small crystal bowls placed to divide segments of groupings, she artfully arranged—or dumped, depending on what mood she was in—handfuls of matchbooks which Mr. Yiplow custom-ordered for the shop. Rarely did the bowls empty, but more than one customer each week did grab a matchbook or two to go with their candle purchases. It didn't surprise Kristin that candles were the shop's best seller; because of the name, most people didn't walk in expecting to buy much else.

Another bowl of matchbooks sat on the counter next to the antique cash register; Kristin often toyed with them as she leaned on the counter when the shop was empty and she was bored. Sometimes she took them all out of the bowl and stacked them into a pyramid like a house of cards. Some days, like today, she would slip them into surprising places throughout the shop: beneath a feathered hat, into the sugar bowl of a china tea set, into the fiddle leaf fig pot by the large front window.

She'd have to retrieve the one from the fig pot later, she realized, because it would be rendered useless as soon as Mr. Yiplow bustled over with his watering can. He was fanatical about caring for that fiddle leaf fig, which he affectionately referred to as Faye, and Kristin speculated that "Faye" had been someone dear to him in his past, for all the care he put into the plant.

He'd been frowning a lot more lately and muttering over the leaves, many of which seemed to be drying and shriveling up no matter how much he watered them, so he'd taken to carrying a silver pair of clippers along with the watering can. With great care he'd snip away the dead leaves and drop them into the wastebasket next to the coffee bar. There'd been so many now it was nearly overflowing, spilling onto the hardwood floor, and Kristin wondered why he hadn't emptied it yet. Perhaps the dead leaves signified a failure which he was determined to correct before moving on from it.

In any case, she'd grab the matchbook in a bit; right now, she had other work to do, and reluctantly she fingered the edge of her textbook, The Microminiature Details of Macroeconomics.

Kristin looked up the instant the bell above the front door jangled, grateful for any interruption, but it was only Donny.

* * *

Wicks 'N' Sticks hosted a rotation of regulars, like Mr. Tran and his six-year-old daughter, a shy girl with almond eyes and thick black bangs always dressed in a black leotard and pink tutu. They came in twice a week after the girl's ballet class so she could pick a small treat. Usually, she chose a piece of candy, but Kristin had noticed she'd deviated last Wednesday to take home a paper doll set.

Mrs. Trimming, an elderly lady who bore a striking resemblance to the queen of England, stopped by nearly as often—once a week, any day of the week, to sniff her way through every candle in no particular order. Kristin still hadn't figured out how she kept track. Between every three candles, she would move to the coffee bar Kristin had set up on a side counter, which Mr. Yiplow constantly muttered about but never objected to, and stick her nose into the canister of whole coffee beans. She never bought anything, but every now and then Kristin saw Mrs. Trimming tuck a matchbook into her cardigan pocket.

No one frequented the shop more than Donny, who came just for the coffee. The thin, bespectacled student spent nearly as much time drinking fresh cups as he did in class at the local university, and in this college town, Kristin knew that when Donny wasn't in the shop, he was likely in class or at the library. She herself spent more time at Wicks 'N' Sticks than she did meandering through her classes. Undecided on a degree, she wasn't holding out for a dream job and always felt distracted. Wicks 'N' Sticks was a good place to be distracted.

Donny caught Kristin's eye, bobbing his head amiably as he walked inside, and she twitched two fingers in a short wave. He was in her economics class, but they weren't friends.

She watched without care as he busied himself grinding some coffee beans and then dropped her gaze to her open textbook. She gave it a hard look for a few seconds, then abruptly flipped the cover closed and shoved the book beneath the countertop.

"If you don't study, Kristina, you will not graduate." Mr. Yiplow wagged a spindly finger in her direction as he emerged from his office. He lowered bushy eyebrows over deep set, dark eyes. "Now, you will look after the shop while I am out, yes? And light one of our new candles for the customers, yes?"

She nodded.

"But—!" and he held up his finger, "—I would have no shop for you to look after nor candles to light had I not studied. You see?"

Kristin shrugged and Mr. Yiplow's frown deepened. He looked at Donny, who pushed his glasses up the bridge of his nose as he examined the coffee beans in the grinder, unaware he was being scrutinized.

"That young man there, Kristina, he studies." Mr. Yiplow nodded in affirmation of his own statement and moved out from behind the counter toward Faye without stopping his scrutiny of Donny. "Young man, I want every coffee ground swept up!"

Donny jumped at Mr. Yiplow's bark and his hand shook as he transferred the grounds to the brewer, spilling some of the coffee across the pristine countertop.

Kristin bit back a laugh as she retrieved her textbook, though she still didn't have any intention of really reading it. She left it lying open next to the register.

Anxious now, Donny fidgeted, drumming the long fingers of one hand against his khakis, eyes glued to the brewer as he waited.

Mr. Yiplow took no notice as he brushed past, and beside the window, took care lifting each of Faye's glossy green leaves to inspect for any blemishes. He harrumphed as soon as he lifted a leaf to find a dry one hidden beneath, and carefully he plucked it off and dropped it on top of the wastebasket. But because the basket was full, that leaf knocked another loose and both toppled down to the floor. There they rested, light brown against the dark wood.

Mr. Yiplow just looked at them, and for a moment his shoulders slumped in defeat. Kristin bit the corner of her lip in concern; she'd never seen him this way before. But he pulled himself up to a straighter height and turned on the heel of his dress shoe to carry on striding out of the shop.

Kristin remembered the matchbook she needed to grab before he returned. Maybe she should also take care of the wastebasket for him.

"Are you ready for the exam?"

Startled, she looked up to find Donny pushing his glasses up his nose right in front of her. A quick glance at the coffee bar confirmed his cup wasn't quite finished brewing.

"Uh. No." Kristin tried to blink away the confusion she felt about his trying to make small talk for the first time. "Um—are you?"

Donny shrugged; his eyes darted away behind his glasses. Was he nervous about the test?

Then he glanced over his shoulder and looked around the shop; when he noticed Mr. Yiplow was gone, he visibly relaxed, dropping his shoulders with a large exhale and pushing up his glasses again. He must not have heard the door.

The corner of Kristin's mouth quirked into a half smile. "Does he make you nervous?"

"You've no idea!" Donny blurted, brown eyes darting around again behind the wire-rimmed oval spectacles. "Like he's just waiting for me to make a mistake or destroy something. Or something."

"He's harmless."

"Maybe." Donny's head bobbed in amiable concession— Kristin wondered whether his neck got tired from all the bobbing his head seemed to do—and looked at the page her textbook was open to. "That's not the exam chapter."

She closed the book and shoved it beneath the counter once more. "Yeah, well. I wasn't exactly studying." She cleared her throat and averted her gaze. "Obviously."

They stood there for several more awkward seconds until she pointed toward the coffee bar. "Think it's done."

"Oh. Oh, yeah—right. Thanks."

Kristin leaned on both elbows and watched Donny transfer the fresh brew into a large to-go cup, carefully fitting a lid over the top and sliding a paper sleeve up the bottom. He picked up a dry napkin and ran it over the counter's surface, sweeping stray coffee grounds to catch with his free hand and brushed his fingers together over the small rattan wastebasket, dropping the napkin on top.

From her perch Kristin couldn't tell whether he'd gotten all the grounds, but it didn't matter; she'd run a damp cloth over the countertop after he'd left and before Mr. Yiplow returned, just to make sure nothing was missed.

Donny picked up his cup, turned in a half circle to salute Kristin with it, and departed.

Idly Kristin plucked a matchbook from the crystal bowl nearby and toyed with it, flipping the cover open and running a fingertip along the neat row of matches with dark blue heads. She'd always thought all matches had red heads until Mr. Yiplow began ordering these.

A grandmother clock for sale in a corner chimed the hour, and she dropped the matchbook back into the bowl and pushed herself off the counter. She wasn't sure what time Mr. Yiplow would be returning, but knew it'd be better if she'd done everything she needed to before then.

She ran a cloth over the coffee counter but Donny had gotten all the grounds, so there was nothing for her to do there except light a candle. Between Donny and Mrs. Trimming, and a handful of others, the coffee bar seemed to get a decent amount of traffic so she'd taken to using it to showcase a new item now and then; plus, having a candle nearby made it seem almost homey, she thought. Like lighting a candle in a kitchen.

She plucked one of the newer spring and summer scents, a blend of orange and champagne called "Monday Morning Mimosa," and took the top off. The name wasn't particularly intriguing, but the candle smelled fresh and a mimosa sounded good.

From the soil Faye was potted in, Kristin pulled the matchbook she buried and brushed off the dirt. It didn't cling as much as she had expected because some of the soil was damp but some was dry. Maybe the fig was soaking up water more quickly than she would've guessed, because Mr. Yiplow did water it often, but that wouldn't explain why half the leaves had been shriveled and dry lately. Maybe Faye was just dying.

Mr. Yiplow never spoke of a wife or family, but maybe "Faye" was named for a wife or a sister or mother who'd passed away, and the state of the leaves reminded him of watching the wife or sister or mother slip away. Maybe that's why his shoulders had drooped so.

But Kristin shook the speculation away; she didn't know anything at all about plants.

Flipping open the matchbook cover and selecting a blue head at random, Kristin swiped it across the striker. A flame ignited, blue fire burning hot where it met the blue head before softening to a cheerful orange glow Kristin touched to the candle's new wick. It, too, ignited, and she blew out the match and dropped it to the wastebasket.

It bounced and fell to the floor as she walked off, landing on a small pile of Faye's dried leaves. Kristin had blown out the open flame but the match head still glowed a smoldering orange—all it took for the leaves to ignite like tinder.

Greedily the flames licked the wood floor and in an instant it caught and began spreading with a terrible rush of wind and crackling; Kristin turned toward the sound and for a second that seemed like an eternity could only watch as the flames rushed across the floor toward her. Then she ran for the counter.

"Fire extinguisher, fire extinguisher," she muttered in a panic, searching. There had to be one. It was an old shop, fully wood-framed, wasn't there some kind of regulation or code that dictated the presence of a fire extinguisher?

There wasn't one beneath or behind the counter, but she spotted a flash of red through Mr. Yiplow's open office door—Yes!

Kristin yanked it up in both hands. It was a small extinguisher and she hoped it would be enough as she aimed the nozzle toward the flames, pulled the pin and depressed the handle.

Nothing happened.

"Come on!" She shook the extinguisher, not knowing whether that would have any effect and tried again—nothing—and gave it a close look. The pressure gauge indicated there wasn't any, and the most recent inspection date on the tag was from the year Kristin was born. "No!"

The flames had spread so quickly across the floor now it would soon be engulfed, and wildly she looked toward windows blocked by merchandise and the front door. The fire had started at the wastebasket near the coffee bar and the fiddle leaf fig, but the door wasn't on fire yet—and it was the only way out, so Kristin sprinted across the burning floor.

* * *

Mr. Yiplow returned while firefighters fought the blaze, which had nearly consumed Wicks 'N' Sticks. He hopped out of his car in hysteria and started for the front door only to be intercepted and manhandled away by two firemen, their faces streaked black from sweat and smoke.

He ended up on his knees on the grass next to Kristin, who was fighting off exhaustion with her back pressed to the tree.

"Kristina," Mr. Yiplow implored, stretching his hands toward her as though begging for alms, "Kristina, please, what happened?"

She could only shake her head and he dissolved into overwhelm and grief, clasping his hands and murmuring.

"No, no, Kristina, Faye... Oh, no, oh dear, Faye..."

Holiday Inn

A J JINKINS III

Holiday Inn Motor Lodge

The faded green carpet of the Holiday Inn Motor Lodge had seen better days, to be sure. Worn out ruts clearly emphasized the higher traffic areas. His eyes mirrored the pale green carpet and he thought to himself, *Holiday Inn, in the old days, would have been a more prestigious option for lodging.* Yet, given his limited resources, this was as good as it gets.

Hobbling in the direction of the front desk, he surveyed the lobby, noting the wallpaper, probably once upon a time a vibrant pastel color, now faded to dull yellow and boasting only stains and smears from years of greasy, oily hands of smokers and children touching it, the bold repetitive patterns now ghosts, barely discernable. The wallpaper, once clinging valiantly to cover its underlayment and bellowing a welcoming greeting to guests, now moaned in agony as it held on feebly to its mooring, losing the battle in several areas.

Limping past the brittle, cracked, leather armchairs and sofas whose cushions sunk in from years of abuse and neglect, he felt the weight of decay that they would feel had they been living beings. He reached the battered wooden check-in desk and stopped to lean against it for support, trying his best to smile despite the sharp pain in his left knee, which his doctors said needed to be replaced again, a procedure he would not allow and could no longer afford.

The bored desk clerk yawned without covering his mouth or apologizing before asking laconically, "May I help you?"

"My name is James Jones, but you can call me Jim. I need a room for one night."

The desk clerk was already staring at his computer, lazily touching keys as if he were having difficulty finding a vacant room at such a late hour as this without a reservation, though the nearly empty parking lot had revealed only a handful of cars occupying spaces in front of rooms.

"I have a room on the ground floor available, Mr. Jones."

They completed the business of financing the room, securing deposits, and informing of amenities. He barely heard the canned blurb from the employee: "The gym is on the second floor to the left. There are ice machines in the middle of the buildings under the stairwells. If you want to swim or relax in the hot tub, the natatorium is located in the center courtyard." *As if it looks like I am going to throw on some swim trunks and take an evening dip!*

Jim slowly made his way to his room, carrying his one soft-side bag by its long strap over his stooped shoulder, wincing with each step as the bag shifted and hit the hip above his bad knee. Passing the middle of the building, he heard the sound of ice dropping in its bay from the machine under the stairwell. *Great! At least the ice machine works,* he thought to himself. With his next step, he discovered that his room was just past the stairwell, and he entered, inserting the key card three times before it worked. Turning on the dim light, he took in his lodging. The musty smell of the spittle of air escaping the ancient unit below the curtained window caught him unawares, and he scrunched up his nose as if to repel the stench. The swaybacked bed, which abutted the wall where the ice machine stood, was the most prominent feature in the dingy space. *Oh well. It will be convenient for me to ice down my knee while I take a nap. I want to be strong and rested for tonight.* Ignoring the scents, he placed his lone bag on the cheap 100- thread-count quilt and immediately laid down next to it. Time for a nap.

The Rusty Pelican

Jim awoke in a startled panic to a clattering sound until he remembered where he was... and why he was disturbed. The ice machine had made another deposit. Dusk had fallen upon his world in the dim room. He could see little in the dark, which revealed only deep shadows and vague silhouettes that threatened to devour him. *Let them have at it,* he thought resignedly for a moment, but then reached over to turn on the side table lamp, which created enough light to cast out the silhouettes, if not all the shadows.

Sitting up and digging into the front pocket of his bag, he slowly pulled out a book of matches, a calling card from brighter days. The worn matchbook was almost forty years old, yet not a single match had been torn from its comb. He stared intently at the cover, reading the advertisement with regret and fondness simultaneously.

The Rusty Pelican
Fresh Seafood and Grog
Where the elite meet in bare feet...

Jim had taken Wendy to the Pelican on their first date nearly 39 years ago. They ate the freshest, most delicious fried snapper, crab, oysters, and shrimp they had ever tasted off of the buffet. When the house band started playing big band music, they hoisted themselves up and danced together around their table, the only diners in the restaurant to take as much pleasure in the music or each other's presence. After they had worn themselves out, and to the applause of the other patrons sitting at their tables, the new couple sat down and quenched their thirsts with margaritas and talked, laughed, and kissed, timidly at first, but with increasing boldness as their feelings and the drinks took control. By the end of the evening, as they closed the joint down, they knew that their destinies were tied together irrevocably. There was no doubt in either of their minds that they would spend their lives by each other's side, raising children to adulthood, serving each other first, community second, sharing good times and bad and seeking comfort in each other's arms through sickness and in health, till death do us part...

Thirty-eight years. We've had quite a run, Wendy. I was always faithful to you, and I know you were to me. We could have a few more years to set the world on fire if only...

He couldn't voice the words. They were too painful to utter, even alone in a dimly-lit room. Wendy changed. Once a fun-loving, joyful, confident woman who would take on the world, she had metamorphosized into a clingy, desperate remora. Perhaps, subconsciously, she knew, but was still trying desperately to hold on to the past. At any rate, he could not allow her to suffer endlessly. She deserved better. A clean break.

He busied himself with the task of preparing to go eat dinner. As he stood naked in the shower, watching the impurities of the day swirl down the drain, he recalled their precious moments fondly, and sorrowful tears joined softly joined the tide. Dried off, dressed, and clean-shaven, he looked about the room once more and caught a glimpse of himself in the mirror. He thought, *You don't look bad, old man. Might even pass for a big spender.* He mentally checked off his list: keys, check; wallet, check . And so on, until he was confident he had forgotten nothing. Turning out the light as he left the room, Jim listened to the click of the door and made his way to the rental car waiting for him ten feet away.

Don's Beachcomber

The Rusty Pelican had long since been torn down, making room for newer, less dated businesses to build up in its place. *Great. It's not even here anymore. I guess the new restaurant will have to be good enough.* Jim went inside, was ushered to a table for one near the kitchen and facilities, and ordered a beer for the first time in years. *Why not go out in style?*

He informed the young, perky waitress he would like the buffet, and she clearly appeared disappointed. Her lips even turned outward into a slight pout. She must have thought he would turn out to be a big tipper, but the buffet would provide less of an opportunity to work him for a gratuity.

Jim ate in silence, lost in his thoughts. With every bite of his fried snapper, each shrimp, each oyster, he recalled a memory from his life with Wendy. Drowning his cavernous sorrow in a third beer, he completed the duty of eating and rose to use the restroom. His left knee was beginning to seize up again. He had not iced it down long enough. Still, as he limped toward the restroom, he imagined Wendy was with him. He raised his arms as if they were dancing together once more, waltzed slowly, haltingly toward his destination.

Bladder relieved, stomach full, and bill paid, being sure to leave a 25% tip for the waitress, he walked through the lobby of Don's Beachcomber. Next to the front door rested a nautical style table with peppermints, individually wrapped toothpicks, and matchbooks advertising the establishment. He picked up a matchbook and read the cover:

Don's Beachcomber
Where good rum is immortalized
And drinking is an art...

Tucking the matches into his pocket, he left to return to the hotel room. His rented bed awaited him. He was exhausted from his travels, and the short afternoon nap had not been long enough. *I get so tired so quickly these days. The cancer is taking over even faster, and even though the doctors said I could live another five years, I know there is not much time left. I only hope I left things well enough for Wendy to keep on going.*

Back at the hotel room, Jim remained dressed in his evening clothes, even leaving his jacket on. He reached for the old matchbook on the nightstand while at the same time retrieving the new Don's Beachcomber one from his pocket. Laying both of them on the bed beside him, he reached into his bag for the bottle of pills the doctors had been prescribing him for the pain in his knee and the pain from his disease. He slowly opened the bottle and looked inside. He had enough.

James Jones, Jim to his friends, swallowed all of the pills in the bottle, chasing them down with the ice water by his bedside. He laid down, head against the mountain of pillows, and wrapped his hand around both matchbooks. The last thing he heard in this world was the sound of the ice machine on the other side of the wall dropping another load into its bin.

Rendezvous

KATHY SIMS

The energy of a busy Friday afternoon at work trans-formed into foreboding of a stagnant evening at home as soon as the clock struck 5 PM. The sudden rustling of papers, closing of drawers, and shuffling of feet signaled Jennifer's co-workers were heading out to homes and families. Unfortunately, she was Cinderella, leaving the excitement of the ball for her cold, lonely hearth.

She smiled and shared wishes for a good weekend with the folks that streamed by her cubicle, lingering, hoping one or two might pause and suggest drinks after work, but no one did. With a silent sigh, she packed up her laptop and locked her desk. Maybe she would do some work this weekend. Whoopie.

Out on the street, the hustle and bustle of New York surrounded her. She loved working in the city, although she couldn't afford to live here. Her mood lifted as she merged with the crowd heading down the subway steps. She didn't have plans yet, but home was a relatively short train ride away and coming back in would be easy. Cheap tickets for

Broadway shows were readily available, there were plenty of museums and sights she hadn't seen and of course, window shopping. Her budget was tight, but she had lots of options. Just solo options.

Forty minutes later, Jennifer disembarked at the Metuchen station. Her salary wouldn't stretch far enough to afford living in New York City, but downtown Metuchen managed the millennial vibe she'd been hoping for. Walking home on Main Street, she decided to stop at Chicks with Chocolate and pick up a treat. Their chocolate was amazing, but her willpower was weak, so she couldn't keep much on hand. Thinking about calories reminded her of exercise. There was a Friday evening hot yoga class, and if she hustled, she could make it. Energized by having a goal, Jennifer picked up her pace as she headed up appropriately named Hillside Drive to her home.

Metuchen Downtown Metro was a small complex, only twenty-four units in an L-shaped building that ran up the hill and across its face. A set of stairs at the beginning of the "L" climbed from the street to a small courtyard nestled in the interior corner. All the units were accessed from this patio, anchored by the communal mailboxes that fronted the few premier parking spots nuzzling along the building.

The bulk of the parking was at the end of a steep driveway that ran behind the long leg of the building. For an expensive, monthly fee, one of these premier interior spots belonged to her. Dad had liked that it was just steps from her front door, for safety reasons. No hiking through dark parking lots for his precious girl.

Jennifer smiled wryly at the tiny patio as she unlocked her mailbox. It was highly doubtful the landlord would ever install the promised furniture and grill. Crossing the small plaza, she waved her key fob at the door to her cluster.

The complex was divided into groups of four that shared a foyer and door to the courtyard. The doors to the first-floor apartments were off to either side of the entrance and a set of stairs ran straight up to a landing for the second-floor units. Each foyer only opened to the key fobs of its cluster and each apartment had a camera feed showing who was ringing for admission. Jennifer's mom had loved these security features.

Flipping through her mail, she stepped to the left and waved the fob at her door. Her apartment was on the first floor, looking out at the parking spots and the roofs or second-story backs of the buildings on Main Street.

Home. Jennifer felt wrapped in a hug just being here. She loved this place, her first solo apartment. She had found it, paid for it, and decorated it, all on her own. No roommates, no clutter, no dirty dishes left in the sink. Slinging the backpack with her laptop onto the end of her gray micro-fiber sofa, just two steps inside the door, she pivoted to close the door.

A small designer chair from a fine furniture store sat in front of the window next to the entry. A splurge for matching throw pillows for her couch tied the pieces together. They were the foretaste of how she intended her future home to look. For now, the rest of the furniture was particle board. The flat screen television sat on a low cabinet opposite the sofa. Her heart warmed, remembering the afternoon she and Dad spent assembling it. Her first particle board project. Two tiny square tables between it and the couch served as both coffee table and footstools. It was convenient that black do-it-yourself furniture matched, regardless of which discount store you bought it from.

She walked the length of the sofa into the kitchen. Wonderful granite countertops with black cabinets anchored the back of the room. Basically, her kitchen started where the sofa ended. Straight ahead was the door to her bedroom with the bathroom tucked just inside. In the righthand corner, past the refrigerator, a door opened onto steps leading down to a surprising bonus basement. It doubled the size of her apartment but was mostly useless. Her laundry was down there, but she lived on the main floor where things were very cozy, but chic.

Grabbing a cup of yogurt from the refrigerator, Jennifer plopped on the couch and propped her feet up on the tiny particle board table. Her brain was telling her to get up, change clothes, and head downtown for yoga. Her emotions were telling her to open the chocolate, pour a glass of wine, and curl up on the couch. Maybe indulge in a little self-pity for how sad it was that such a successful, pretty, young woman like herself was home alone on a Friday night.

It was kind of amusing to envision the angelic good girl on her right shoulder argue with the devilish naughty girl on her left shoulder about exercising and indulging. As she finished her snack, the good girl was winning, when her phone started buzzing. The group text was exploding with messages from Katie and Theresa, her former college roommates.

"Jennifer, happy Fri-yay!"

"Wish we were there, or you were here."

Jennifer smiled as she texted back. "Me too."

"Heading into the city? Going to see a show? Cruise around Times Square?" Theresa had such grandiose ideas of what a Friday night in New York could be like.

"Or are you hunkering down at home to unwind?" Katie knew Jennifer a little better.

Although Jennifer was sure she meant it in a nice way, it still stung a little to think that was what Katie expected her to be doing.

"Haven't decided. What are you two wild women up to?"

"Headed to House of Blues. One of the guys at work is in a band that's the opening act tonight," Katie texted. "Never heard of the main group, but he gave me tickets."

"Sounds like fun," Jennifer replied. "What type of music?"

"Later," Katie came back. "We need to grab our tickets from will-call and get in line. No chairs you know, so we want a spot where we can at least lean against the wall."

"Have fun," Jennifer texted. "Tell me all about it to-morrow."

"Will do." Smiley emoji from Katie.

Thumbs up from Theresa.

Jennifer sent back a group hug emoji, then dropped the phone on the couch beside her. She stared bleakly at the black television screen as the good girl/bad girl voices in her head started arguing again. Glancing at the time on her phone, she knew she could still make the class if she hurried.

Suddenly a tidal wave of the blues washed across her, sweeping away the arguments about what to do. Her friends were going out together, doing something fun. She was stuck here all by herself. Alone. Nothing to do except sit on the couch and binge watch Netflix. Tears filled her eyes and trembled on her lashes.

The hell with it. Jennifer dragged her backpack across the couch to her and dug the chocolate box out. Taking a bite of the hazelnut truffle, she wiped her eyes and leaned back. It wasn't fair. When she'd first told her friends that she'd gotten a job in New York, they'd been so excited. They'd talked about girls' weekends in the city, taking in the shows, the sights, the shopping. Plans to take driving trips to see the fall foliage in New England. Winter skiing in the Poconos. Jennifer's apartment was going to be the launch pad for hundreds of amazing adventures.

She popped the rest of the truffle in her mouth, sadness and self-pity souring the sweetness. Melancholy coalesced into resentment as she remembered those castles in the sky. After graduation, all these plans evaporated. Jennifer did her part, making the move, getting her apartment, even buying a foldup memory foam mattress so her friends could sleep in comfort when they came.

But Katie and Theresa didn't follow through. Katie's parents encouraged her to buy a starter home rather than rent, so suddenly her cash flow was tight. She couldn't seem to manage a couple hundred dollars to fly to New York, although she talked about setting aside money for a European vacation over the holidays. No New Years in Times Square this year.

Theresa was suffering from what the media called "failure to launch." She was still living in their college apartment, rooming with her younger sister and her friends. Struggling to get motivated to find a job or apply to graduate school, she was biding her time, working at Target. Maybe she still wanted to come but knew there was no way she could afford it. Maybe if Jennifer paid for her ticket. And her meals. And her souvenirs.

Jennifer snorted. Was she so pathetic that she had to pay for people to be her friends? Setting aside the chocolate box, she pulled her laptop out of her backpack and fired it up. When she'd moved here, her parents had suggested finding a church, looking for groups that shared her interests, volunteering. Try different things until she found one that clicked.

She had tried. Visited a couple churches and had been excited about one that offered a study group called Bible and Brews. According to the website, the group met at local breweries to discuss theology and try new beers. She'd even gone to one session, only to discover it was a group of married men. They'd welcomed her warmly and encouraged her to come back, but it just wasn't what she was looking for.

Depending on which yoga classes she attended, there were a few young professional women that she'd begun chatting with, but they hadn't progressed to the "let's get together" stage.

Drumming her fingers on her computer, Jennifer thought. What kind of things did she like to do? Go to shows, hike, shop, check out breweries, drink coffee...hmm. Clicking through several Meetup lists, nothing appealed to her. Frustrated, she typed "how to meet young professionals in Metuchen" into Google and clicked the search button.

Good old Google always has an answer. The top result was a sponsored ad for speed dating. *OMG was she that desperate?* No one would know if she just looked at it. Embarrassed but curious, Jennifer clicked on the link.

"Welcome to First Dates!" the banner proclaimed. The website had a photo of an attractive couple smiling over drinks with a short paragraph describing how their service allowed you to meet single professional men and women safely in lounges, restaurants, and other upscale venues in the Metuchen area. "We have the highest quality singles you can find" the site assured. "Join us at an upcoming event to experience it for yourself." Jennifer started to close the ad, then hesitated. It wouldn't hurt to at least see how it worked. It wasn't like she had anything else going on.

Huh. There was a dating session tonight. Her fingers tippy tapped lightly on the keys as she debated. *Try something new or stay with the comfortable, boring routine? Risk meeting people or sit home alone?*

She stared at the "Create an Account" button. *What the heck. It would be an adventure.*

After a somewhat frantic ninety minutes spent building a profile and stressing over what to wear, Jennifer headed out to her car, dressed, not quite to the nines, but nicely. Her floral dress was perky and flounced above her knees. She'd covered the spaghetti straps with a pale pink shrug, both for warmth and to cover up a bit. She wanted to look pretty, but not too sexy. Strappy white sandals and a small clutch finished her look.

The First Date event was being held in the Crystal Ballroom at the Radisson Hotel in Edison, the donut town that encircled Metuchen, the hole in the donut. In fifteen minutes, Jennifer had parked and was strolling through the lobby, following signs to a cloth-covered table outside a large ballroom. A cheerful middle-aged woman exuding mom vibes smiled up at her as she approached.

"Hello, welcome to First Dates. I'm Martha. Have you attended one of our events before?"

"Uh, no," Jennifer said.

"Well, that cute sweater is a perfect choice. Sometimes these hotel conference rooms can get cold after a while."

Martha patted the pale blue sweater she was wearing over (*OMG!*) a navy floral shirtdress.

Jennifer did a mental facepalm. *I look like a mini-Martha. I should just go home.*

"Did you register online?" Martha cocked her head like a curious bird, waiting for Jennifer's now-reluctant nod.

"Great. Do you have your ID number?

Nodding again, Jennifer felt like a mute bobblehead. Doomed to see this through.

"Perfect." The woman pushed a name tag and a marker towards Jennifer. "Write your first name on this tag." Next Martha handed her a card. "Write your ID number in the top right-hand corner here." She pointed. "Tonight is Ladies night, which means that you will stay seated at your table while the gentlemen move from one table to the next. When a man sits down, you exchange ID numbers. You'll have 5 minutes to chat, then the chime will sound. The gentleman will stand up to move, and you'll have about a minute to write a score beside his number."

"What kind of scoring system?" Jennifer asked, suddenly anxious.

"You can use any scale you like," said Martha. "It's just for your benefit, so that at the end of the evening you can rank the men you've met. When the evening is over you circle the ID numbers of the gentlemen you'd be interested in seeing for a second date." Martha smiled reassuringly at her. "We collect the cards and enter only the selected IDs in our system. If you and a gentleman both indicate an interest in each other, we will send a Second Date email giving you each other's First Dates' email addresses. After that, it's up to you to reach out to each other."

Martha looked up at Jennifer somewhat sternly. "Do you remember the guidelines you were required to read before registering? Being careful about how much personal information you share initially, and making sure you set up your second date in a public place?" Jennifer nodded again. She felt like she was talking to a guidance counselor. "Good. We do screen people, but you are responsible for your safety and privacy." Martha gave her a brilliant smile. "You're all set. Go on in and Mark will set you up at a table."

Feeling a little overwhelmed, Jennifer stepped into the ballroom. Round covered tables were set up throughout the room, spaced just far enough apart to offer the illusion of privacy for conversation. Each table had a number, and several had attractive young women already seated at them. A group of men hung awkwardly in the back of the room, standing close together, but not talking, each holding a card. A young man in a red polo shirt with the First Dates logo stepped up to her. His name tag read "Mark."

"Hi there. Come with me and we'll find you a table." Jennifer felt herself blushing and kept her eyes on Mark's shoes as she followed him across the room to a table with a number eight sign. "Here you are." Mark smiled. "Have a seat and get comfortable. We'll be starting in a few minutes. Good luck tonight."

Jennifer sat down and tucked her purse in her lap. Fidgeting with her card, she took furtive glances around the room. It felt too awkward to look at the men, like walking through an animal rescue, feeling desperate, hopeful eyes trying to meet your gaze. Instead, she studied the women at the other tables.

Most appeared to be slightly older than Jennifer, maybe in their late thirties based on the quality of their clothing, the designer bags beside their chairs, and their calm confidence assessing the cluster of men. A few seemed to be her age. Young women dressed nicely, but nervously avoiding eye contact with everyone. She wished she could just skip meeting the men and get to know these women. A girlfriend to hang out with had a lot more appeal than a date.

Crap. She needed a pen for her rankings. Jennifer fumbled with her purse, wondering if she had one. With increasing alarm, she dug through her little bag, Nothing. She started looking desperately around the room, wondering if she was going to have to borrow a pen from one of these other women. The competition.

Phew. Martha had entered the ballroom, closing the door, and was going from table to table with a fistful of ballpoint pens. Jennifer sagged with relief. It looked like Mark was handing some out to the men. When Martha reached table eight, she handed Jennifer one. "Give it a quick scratch to test it, dear. Sometimes they dry out." Anxiously Jennifer scribbled on the corner of her card. It worked. Martha gave her an encouraging smile. "Aren't you glad you have your sweater? It's definitely chilly in here tonight."

Jennifer rubbed her arms and nodded. Martha beamed at her. "Relax and have fun," she chirped, moving on.

A melodious chime sounded loudly in the room. The nervous shuffling ceased, and Mark addressed the room. "Ladies and gentlemen, welcome to First Dates. That chime is the sound you'll hear when it's time to stop and start your conversations. When I sound the chime, gentlemen move to your assigned starting table and begin. The next time you hear it, you will say your goodbyes and head to your next table. Take a moment to mark your cards, then move on. Ladies, you don't need to move tonight, but do be sure to mark your card before your next date sits down." Mark looked down at his notes. "We have a nice sized group tonight, so you won't get a chance to meet everyone. Just enjoy the folks you get to chat with." He lifted his eyes and gazed around the room. "Ready?" The chime sounded.

Jennifer wiped her hands surreptitiously on her dress. Her first date sat down. Khakis, blue button-down shirt, glasses, average brown hair. Typical corporate low-rung guy. *A pocket protector? Seriously?*

"Hi, I'm Dwight, ID number 9411."

"Uh, hi, I'm Jennifer, number 9542."

"Nice to meet you Jennifer," Dwight said as he wrote down her number. Belatedly, Jennifer realized she needed to write his down and she'd already forgotten it.

"I'm sorry, Dwight, I'm a little nervous. This is my first speed dating event, and I, uh, forgot your number."

"No problem," he chuckled. "It's 9411."

"Thanks," she said and carefully noted it. She looked up to see him watching her. "Um, have you done this before?"

"Yeah, I've been to a couple. It's kind of a neat way to find people."

"Have you had any second dates?" Jennifer smacked her face mentally. "Oh, I'm sorry, that's none of my business."

Dwight shrugged. "It's okay. I've gone on a few. I enjoy meeting fresh faces."

"Oh. That's nice." Jennifer winced mentally. She sounded like an old maid auntie. They managed a few more clunky exchanges, Jennifer mentally begging the chime to *please* sound at each awkward pause. At long last the soft bong came.

"Nice meeting you Jennifer."

"You too Dwight."

Oh my god. That was only the first one. How many more do I have to get through? Why on earth did I decide to do this? Never, ever, ever again. She just had to survive tonight.

As the next man sat down at her table, Jennifer remembered she had to give Dwight a rating. Ugh. One star. She'd do a scale of one to five stars, with five being great.

"Hello there. I'm Frank." Flustered by almost forgetting to score Dwight, poor Frank was just a nerve-racked blur, blending into the muffled pulse of conversations from the other tables.

Thirty minutes later, Jennifer was finally getting the hang of it. The first two dates had been excruciating, but the third guy was actually easy to talk with. They had seen several of the same Broadway shows and discussed what they wanted to see next. Jennifer gave him four stars. He seemed like he might be worth a second date. Maybe. She was a little sorry when the chime sounded, sending him on his way.

"Hello beautiful. I can't believe someone as lovely as you would be at a speed date." A cloud of musky cologne almost choked her.

Jennifer looked up with a forced smile, holding her breath. Definitely one star with that opening line. Mr. Cologne looked to be her dad's age, dressed in what must have been cool when he was young. Her heart twisted as she imagined her father struggling to meet women if her mom was gone, but misplaced pity was not going to win him a second date with her.

Finally, the double chime sounded, and Mark addressed the room again. "Ladies and gentlemen, that's all the time we have tonight. Please be sure to mark the dates you're interested in seeing again. If we find a match, we'll send you both contact information. Thank you for coming. Good-night and drive safely."

Jennifer rolled her shoulders and stretched out her feet. She was exhausted. It was amazing how much work an hour's worth of small talk was. Looking down at her card, she wondered if it had been worth it. Date number three, Stephen, had been the only one the least bit interesting.

Tapping her pen on the card a few times, Jennifer thought about the painful conversations she'd endured. *One out of six. Was that typical? Had Stephen really been good enough for a second date? Was she being too picky?* Tap, tap, tap. *What the heck, it was worth a shot.* She circled his ID number, stood up and headed for the door. Time to go home and treat herself to another truffle. She'd earned a reward this evening.

* * *

Saturday morning, Jennifer really wanted to sleep in, but Little Big Foot, the toddler that lived above her with his parents, had gotten up early and was driving trucks across the floor. Loudly. Eventually she heard the family clomping down the steps, but by then she was wide awake, unable to go back to sleep. The sun was shining, so rather than make coffee at home, Jennifer decided to walk down to Brewed Awakening for some avocado toast and a latte. Thanks to Little Big Foot, she was early enough to beat the weekend crowd and claim a table. Scrolling through social media updates on her phone, she relaxed and enjoyed her breakfast.

Instagram had a new selfie of Katie and Theresa at the House of Blues last night. Having a blast. Without her.

Melancholy washed over her, dimming the bright morning momentarily.

Snap out of it! Jennifer scolded herself. Wait until she told them how she'd spent her Friday night. They'd flip out. Well, if she told them. Maybe if she got a second date, she'd tell them.

Jennifer straightened in alarm. *What if Stephen, date number three, didn't select her for a follow up?* Oh my god, there was no way she was telling her friends about speed dating unless she got a second date.

Suddenly stressed, Jennifer checked her phone. The email icon showed two new messages. Opening the app, Jennifer saw the earlier message was from First Dates. "Congratulations, you and Stephen connected during the recent speed dating event. Your First Dates' contact links are below so you can reach out to each other. Please review the guidelines on our website before setting up a date. Remember, you are responsible for your safety and privacy. We hope you have a wonderful Second Date."

Thank God I didn't fail. Sipping her latte, Jennifer was a little shocked at how relieved she felt. It would have been awful to go through all that and not find a match.

The second message was from Stephen. "Hi Jennifer. I'm glad you are interested in a second date with me. You were so easy to talk to, I really felt like we connected. I would like to see you again and was hoping it wouldn't be too pushy if I suggested meeting for dinner tonight. I know an excellent restaurant in Woodbridge called the Landmark Inn. If you're available, I'll make reservations."

Wow. Jennifer swallowed the last bite of her toast. She was feeling a little giddy. It had worked. She'd gone speed dating and found a guy she thought she might like who thought he might like her. Clearing her table for the next customer, she started walking home, sipping her coffee.

Now what? Did she really want to meet him for dinner? So far, he only had her email address from the First Date site. If she had dinner with him, he might want her phone number. Of course, she could always say no. If she was brave enough. Sometimes her desire to please people overwhelmed her good sense. Back in her apartment, Jennifer looked around at her four wonderful walls. It seemed like her choices were the same as last night's. Stay home alone with the television or put herself out there and try to meet people. She'd come this far; she might as well go one step further.

"Stephen, I'd love to join you for dinner this evening. Just let me know what time and the name the reservation will be under. I'm looking forward to getting to know you. Jennifer."

Send.

Jennifer stared at her phone for a few moments, then laughed at herself. It would be stupid of her to sit around waiting for a new email to come in. She stood up and stretched. Dirty dishes and dirty clothes were calling her name.

Ping.

She grabbed her phone. A new email. From Stephen. *That was fast. Was it too fast? Had he changed his mind?*

Chewing her lip, Jennifer opened the message. "Great! Our reservations are for seven under the name Stephen Durum. See you tonight."

Okay then. A goofy grin spread across her face. She definitely needed to do some laundry. And get her nails done. And look up directions to the Landmark Inn. Jennifer felt excitement fluttering in her stomach. This could be good. Perhaps the start of something. Sternly, she gave herself a mental shake.

Stephen was still a stranger. All her parents' warnings about stranger danger flooded in. She needed to be careful. Stay calm, be smart, and take things slow. That's what she would do. But she couldn't help skipping a little as she gathered up her laundry.

* * *

The evening was clear and beautiful, a crescent moon and the first star shining in the sky. Maybe it was a sign. Jennifer made a wish for a nice date, followed by a quick prayer that she would be mindful of her safety. By the time she reached the Landmark Inn, the sky had darkened to a deep navy hue, which complimented the inn's blue peaked roof. This was more than just a restaurant. It was a conference center with a luxurious pool sporting white statuary and several fountains. Jennifer had arrived a few minutes early to allow herself time to park, but it was such a large facility, she decided to use the valet service. This gave her time to freshen up and soothe her nerves.

She'd opted for a classic little black dress and pearls tonight. Assessing her look in the ladies' room mirror, Jennifer touched up her lip gloss to calm her nerves. She liked the successful young professional woman she saw. Precisely at 7 PM, she approached the maître d' and gave the reservation.

"Right this way, madam." She followed the dark suit through the elegant dining room to a semi-secluded table overlooking the pool. Stephen was already there, and he rose as she approached. He had dressed up as well, wearing charcoal gray slacks, a matching shirt, and a stark black tie. The monochrome look suited his dark hair and eyes, and gray avoided washing out his fair complexion to pasty goth. A little tingle ran through Jennifer as she thought about what an attractive couple they made.

"Jennifer, it's so nice to see you again." He extended his hand, so she shook it. The maître d' pulled out her chair and she sat somewhat self-consciously. Stephen took his chair after she was seated. "I'm glad you were available tonight. I really didn't want to wait a week or more for the opportunity to get better acquainted." He gazed at her intently.

A little flustered, Jennifer smiled and gazed out at the pool. "I was happy to hear from you. This is a lovely place."

"The food is wonderful too. I know you'll enjoy it."

The waiter arrived to describe the daily specials and take their drink orders. Jennifer decided to start with water, although Stephen ordered a bottle of merlot for them to share with dinner. After they had placed their orders, New York strips with the usual accompaniments for them both, he picked up their discussion about Broadway shows from the night before. Jennifer began to relax a little as they found the easy flow of conversation again.

The steaks were delicious, and when Jennifer declined dessert, Stephen suggested they move to the bar for a digestif drink. There was a lively group at one end of the bar, so they selected a quieter table across the room. Stephen ordered a brandy, but Jennifer was feeling just a bit fuzzy from the wine she'd had with dinner. Attentive Stephen had been very courteous, keeping her glass topped off.

"Jennifer, please don't make me drink alone," he said, pulling a mock pouty face. He looked so much like a grumpy little boy, that she relented and ordered an Amaretto on the rocks. The cool ice balanced the burn of the alcohol on her lips.

It was nice, she thought gazing around, *genuinely nice, to be out on a date with a man who was polite, attractive, and easy to be with. I'd forgotten that dates could be fun.* On the table was an ashtray, holding a matchbook, folded to stand up like a tiny tent. It was a bright blue, with "Rendezvous Lounge" in white script on one side, and "Landmark Inn" on the other. To Jennifer's delight, the tips of the matches were also blue. *This is a perfect souvenir,* she thought, tucking it into her purse.

The crew at the bar was getting louder. A twenty-something blonde, who may have had too much to drink, was laughing with abandon. She had pushed herself up to sit on the bar, her red sheath creeping up her thighs and her feet resting on the barstool. A brunette and a couple of men were with her, downing shots. The bartender was ignoring them, but Stephen seemed intrigued by the scene.

Jennifer tried to start a conversation, but it seemed that every time she spoke, the blonde's boozy laugh would ring out and Stephen's eyes would flick her way. Annoyed, Jennifer excused herself and went to the powder room.

Away from the noise of the bar, she could tell that she'd had more to drink tonight than she'd planned. *I'm still okay to drive*, she thought, as she looked in the mirror, brushing her hair back and touching up her lips. *But I think it's time to call it a night.* She tilted her head. *Should I give him my phone number if he asks? Do I want to see him again?*

Dinner had been good. It was when they moved to the bar, Jennifer realized, that she'd begun to feel a bit uncomfortable. That little bit of pressure to keep drinking. His obvious interest in the inebriated blonde. She dropped her brush into her purse. Time to go home. She was willing to see him again, but she would stick to email contact for now. She knew his last name from the reservation, but she hadn't shared hers yet (following First Dates' guidelines for second dates). She smiled at her reflection. Maybe they could see a show or something for a third date.

How many dates do you have to take before you stop numbering them? Jennifer wondered.

Heading back to the bar, Jennifer paused at the doorway. The bartender had approached the tipsy woman and was pointing at the barstool, obviously asking her to get off the bar. Instead, she was attempting to stand up on it. Her girlfriend was tugging on her hand, trying to pull her down, but the guys were cheering her on. Jennifer shook her head. Definitely time to go home. She made a wide loop around the perimeter of the room to avoid the scene and ended up approaching her table on an angle from behind Stephen.

He was no longer staring at the blonde and her friends. A fresh round of drinks sat on in front of him, and as she drew nearer, she saw him drop something into her glass. He picked it up and swirled it several times, setting the drink down just as she reached the table. She paused, disturbed.

Sensing her presence, he looked up at her startled. "Where did you come from? I thought the restrooms were just down the bar?"

Jennifer forced herself to stay calm. "They are. I just took the long way around to avoid the rowdy group at the end."

Stephen stood to pull out her chair. "Smart move. They seem to be getting a bit out of hand."

Feeling uneasy, Jennifer remained standing. "Stephen, I hate to end this so abruptly, but the noise has given me a headache. I'm sorry, but I need to go home."

He frowned slightly. "We could take our drinks out by the pool. It would be a lot more peaceful out there." He moved to pick up both glasses.

"No, I'm sorry. Once my head starts hurting, I just need to go home." She tried to keep the quiver out of her voice. Telling someone "No" always felt rude, and she liked people to like her.

"Is it safe for you to drive?" Stephen was all solicitous concern. "I could take you home and help you get your car sometime tomorrow."

"I'll be fine. It was a lovely evening. Thank you." She tucked her clutch under her arm, and crossed her arms at her waist, giving herself a hug for courage. Jennifer edged towards the door, trying to end the conversation. Stephen took a step towards her.

"Let me at least walk you to your car. It wouldn't be appropriate for me to let you wander the parking lot at night alone, especially when you have a headache."

"That's very thoughtful, Stephen, but please stay and finish your drink. I did valet parking, so they'll bring my car around."

Reaching out to take her hand, Stephen looked into her eyes. "I enjoyed this evening very much. Are you sure you can get home safely? Will you give me your number so I can call to make sure you made it?

Jennifer hesitated. He seemed so sincere and thoughtful. Dinner had been so nice. Then she thought about him swirling her drink, and her resolve strengthened. "I'll send you an email when I get home Stephen. You can check it on your phone."

His grip on her hand tightened slightly, but she pulled it away and forced a bright smile. "You know Martha gave me quite a lecture last night about the Second Date guidelines. I wouldn't want to disappoint her by disobeying them on my first second date." She managed a small chuckle, and he grinned back reluctantly.

"You're right, we don't want to end up on Martha's bad side."

They laughed together and Jennifer stepped away. "Goodnight Stephen."

"Until next time, Jennifer."

In your dreams, she thought, although she kept a smile on her face until she was out of the bar. She glanced back a couple times as she crossed the lobby, unreasonably anxious, to make sure he wasn't following her. When she reached the valet stand, she told them she'd wait outside, pointing to a large planter just past the doors. Her car wouldn't be visible there when she got in.

Driving home, Jennifer's head started to ache for real, and she began to tremble. The primal part of her brain was worried, as if it sensed a predator. Repeatedly checking the rearview mirror didn't help, because she had no way of knowing if someone was tailing her. By the time she reached Metuchen, Jennifer was so distraught, she missed her turn and ended up crawling through the downtown weekend traffic before reaching a corner that allowed her to circle back. The road was dark as she came down the hill to the driveway, and she breathed a sigh of relief. After parking, she got her fob out of her purse and held it ready. Dashing the short distance to her door, she swiped herself into the foyer, then turned and yanked the door shut. Pivoting quickly, she opened her door, jumped inside, slammed it closed. She stood, shaking. Home. Safe.

Shuddering, Jennifer flipped the wall switch to turn off the table lamp she'd left on and peeked out the blinds at the small parking lot. No other cars pulling in. She pressed her car's remote lock and saw the taillights flash. Her head pounding, she felt her way to the bathroom in the dark, trailing her fingers along the back of the couch as a guide. In the bathroom, she used the glow of her cell phone to find some aspirin and brush her teeth.

She followed the wall to her closet, changing into pajamas in the dark, then peered out the bedroom blinds at the driveway. All quiet. Huddled under her blankets, Jennifer fearfully listened for the sounds of cars approaching, or strangers creeping. After a very long time, she fell into a fitful sleep.

* * *

The next morning, Jennifer woke to the pounding sounds of Little Big Foot running through the apartment upstairs. Her head still hurt. It felt like the beginning of a migraine, probably triggered by the sulfites in the red wine from the night before. She dragged herself out of bed long enough to use the restroom, take some headache medicine and grab some water. Then she nestled back down into her blankets.

While waiting for the medication to kick in, she pulled out her phone. Her stomach lurched. An email from Stephen.

"Didn't hear from you last night. Please let me know you made it home safely. Stephen."

She closed her eyes in embarrassment. Safe at home, in the bright, reasonable light of day, Jennifer was sure she had misinterpreted Stephen's handling of her drink and his fascination with the drunk woman. Pulling the covers over her head, she just wanted to curl up in a ball of humiliation and die. She was never going to be able to face him again. Why had she gotten so freaked out? How much of that wine had she drunk? At least he only had her first name and the First Dates' email address. She would just delete her account and never, ever, *ever*, go speed dating again.

Feeling slightly better now that she had a plan for avoiding Stephen for all eternity, Jennifer plumped her pillows and sat back, tapping on her news app. She liked the tabs it had at the top for National News, Politics, Local, and Weather. Selecting the Local tab, she resolved to look for better ways to make connections with her community. Maybe volunteering somewhere.

As the page opened, she grimaced. The lead story was a body. A young woman had been found floating in the pool of a local hotel. Cause of death was under investigation. Jennifer lifted her finger to scroll past, then froze as the picture loaded.

It was the drunk blonde from the bar.

Suburbia Inn

CORINNA SEE

As usual, Francie was freezing, and she wondered—not for the first time—what had possessed her to take the job.

She spun a matchbook on the desk in front of her, staring absentmindedly toward the fireplace. No matter how ardently she stoked it, no matter how warm and cheery the blaze, the living room lobby always felt cold. The entire house felt cold.

The matchbook was supposed to be a souvenir for visitors—not that there ever were any. It was one the reason she'd accepted the offer to be the proprietor of the Suburbia Inn, a bed and breakfast-style establishment in a house that looked more like it belonged in a storybook than in the heart of Suburbia. No one ever visited Suburbia.

Instead, Francie had taken to hoarding the matchbooks in a desk drawer. She went through them so quickly, rekindling the fire and tinkering with the ornery old furnace that belched more black smoke than it did warmth.

She flipped open the top to see how many matches were left in this one. Three. One for the fireplace, one for the furnace, and one to burn the old Victorian to the ground.

Francie half-smiled at her own cynicism. She actually liked the house—always wanted to live in one just like it. And the job wasn't even bad; it was easy, and she liked easy. It was quiet. Paid well and afforded her plenty of time to read the horror novels she couldn't quite get enough of.

If only she'd known how *cold* she would feel.

With a sigh, she slid off the stool, shoving the match-book into her sweater pocket, only to take it out again as soon as she reached the fireplace, which crackled dully.

Francie wadded up some newspaper and used a poker to shove it into the embers. She struck a match and touched the dancing flame to the tip of the paper, which smoldered and curled as it caught. Then she fed the blaze with several dry logs, enough to last through the night, tossing in another match for good measure. When the fire flared, and she dusted off her hands, closed the mesh wire curtain, and tucked the matchbook back into her pocket.

"There," she said to the empty room. "That should do."

In the hall, the grandfather clock on the staircase landing *bonged* seven times. Francie turned off the overhead light and flicked on the check-in desk lamp, which met the light of the fire in a cozy glow.

Time to lock up.

After flipping the "Open" sign to "Closed" in the foyer window, Francie headed down the hall to the proprietor's suite: a small bedroom attached to an even smaller bath-room. Both were minimally furnished, with little more than an antique four-poster bed, a slipper chair upholstered in velvet brocade, and an antique vanity between them. She dragged the heavy down comforter off the bed and wrapped it around her slight frame as she trudged back to the warmth of the fire.

Francie shoved an armchair as close to the hearth as she could manage and curled up in it, pulling the comforter around her.

The next time Francie's eyes opened, she blinked, unsure that they were really open in the dark.

The lamp was off. The fire was out.

With a sigh, she pulled the matchbook from her pocket and opened it, fumbling the last match with chilled, stiff fingers. She dropped it on the tattered rug without any inkling of where it landed and, with a groan of frustration, she fell to her hands and knees to blindly grope around for it.

When her fingers closed around the slim piece of wood, she struck the head along the booklet's rough stripe, igniting a tiny flame.

Francie held the light out in front of her. It didn't illuminate much; she could only just make out the shape of furniture to avoid as she moved toward the lamp on the desk. She flicked the switch. Nothing happened.

She tried again; still nothing.

Probably a tripped breaker or a blown fuse, Francie thought, fending off annoyance. *Could be anything in this damn house.*

With the lamp out of commission, she tried the wall switch for the room; when that, too, failed to shed some light on her situation, she started for the fireplace. The match flame singed her fingertips.

"Ow!" Francie dropped the match, shaking out her hand and sucking on her thumb and forefinger. "Shit."

Rendered blind once more, she rooted around in the desk for a fresh matchbook. Was this the right drawer? No. *It's fine, there should be at least one in the top drawer...* Pens rattled and scraps of notepad paper rustled as Francie dug around in the mess. When finally her fingers closed around the slender booklet, she rekindled the fire, until the heat warmed her cheeks and she could breathe in the scent of wood smoke.

A power outage wouldn't affect the furnace—which had probably gone out again anyway—but would need to be fixed as soon as possible. A tripped breaker, she could fix, but if it was more than that, she would have to call somebody in the morning.

"I *tried* to tell the owners to invest in a back-up generator," she muttered, rummaging through the check-in desk for a flashlight.

The flashlight beam was dim, but glowed just enough that she could make out the furnishings as she moved into the hallway: the staircase facing the open front door, the small table placed against the flocked wallpaper, the coat and umbrella rack devoid of coats and umbrellas.

Francie beamed the light briefly over everything, shivering as a wintry chill blew through her sweater, and turned automatically toward the basement door down the hall.

Wait.

She moved the flashlight beam back through the small foyer.

Hadn't she locked the front door?

Francie frowned. Nibbled at the inside of her cheek; felt automatically for the matchbook in her pocket—though what purpose it would serve away from the fireplace and the furnace, she had no idea. It simply comforted her to know it was there.

The "Closed" sign looked back at her, meaning the sign in the window advertised an open establishment; maybe she hadn't locked up after all, and the wind had just blown the front door ajar, as it was wont to do with the latch loose as it was.

She changed the sign and shut the door firmly, pulling on the knob to make sure it was completely closed before engaging the deadbolt.

"There. That should hold."

* * *

Of the entire house, Francie most disliked the basement —not least because it was where the chill seemed to emanate from.

Unfinished, it was simply a storage space that the owners had filled with whatever they'd accumulated over time and no longer wanted to display in the house: a harpsichord with broken keys, a dressmaker's mannequin, an assortment of fake plants and dated furniture. An odd hodgepodge, all of it together, with half the items covered in ghostly white sheets, although she could never figure out what they were being preserved for.

She lingered on the stairs for a moment, indulging in the ghoulish fantasy of the mannequin growing taller beneath its sheet, which whispered in an icy breeze...

Francie shivered in the stagnant air, shaking the frightening image from her mind. Her short red curls stirred up lingering dust motes, and she sneezed. Something skittered on the far side of the room, and she forced her attention to her objective so as not to think wildly.

The breaker box was next to the furnace, which, indeed, also required attention. *Well, first things first*—she opened the breaker panel and ran her finger down the row of switches, searching for one that was not like the others.

There wasn't one.

She sighed. It must have been a power outage, then, and there was nothing she could do about that, particularly not at this time of night.

As if on cue, the grandfather clock distantly *bonged* many times to remind her of how late it was. If Francie had any hope of opening up on time in the morning, she would need to get to bed soon.

She closed the breaker box and glanced toward the furnace. For a moment, it seemed to glare back at her, and a brief vision flashed before her eyes of the mouth yawning open wide enough to suck her in like a black hole and swallow her down, down, into the fiery depths of the Hell that used to terrify her on Sundays.

Francie swallowed, then drew in a breath and squared her shoulders. "Stop it, Francesca. It's just a furnace. There's absolutely nothing to be afraid of."

Still, she worked a little more hurriedly than usual to get it going again, barely bothering to wipe the grime from her hands when she finished before grabbing her flashlight and taking the steps two at a time up the stairs.

Francie slammed the basement door shut behind her and leaned against it, breathing heavily in relief. The hallway was dim and unlit, but she could hear the fire still crackling reassuringly in the next room, and the front door was still closed.

She laughed, suddenly, at how ridiculous she was being.

"Silly stupid girl," she chided herself. "It's just an old house, in an old neighborhood in the middle of *Suburbia*, of all places. There's absolutely *nothing* to be afraid of!"

"Yes, Francesca," whispered a voice next to her ear, and Francie's blood turned to ice. "There's nothing to be *afraid* of."

In the next instant, one hand clamped over her nose and mouth, another arm wrapped around her throat, and Francie struggled uselessly as everything faded to black.

* * *

The next time Francie's eyes opened, she blinked, unsure that they were really open in the dark.

The lamp was off. The fire was out.

Super 6 Motel

KATHY SIMS

"We won't leave the light on," Mark sneered as he opened the motel room door.

The room beyond was a cave, pitch black and quiet. Just enough light from the breezeway spilled in through the entrance to show the worn carpet and allow him to fumble for the light switch. Mark checked both directions on the dusty sidewalk. Empty. Good. He heaved the duffle bag at his feet across the threshold, stepped through, spun, closed, and locked the door. A smooth, graceful sequence, like steps in a dance. Until his heel clipped his bag and he fell sideways, catching himself on the wall with a thud.

"Smooth move," he muttered.

Shoving off the wall, Mark slumped across the room to the queen bed, turned and flopped backwards onto it as if it were a pool. He closed his eyes for a few moments, then propped himself up on his elbows to survey his temporary home.

The motel room was smaller than his old bedroom in his parents' home. Across the narrow walkway at the foot of the bed was the standard stretch of built-ins: a desk with a rolling chair, a three-drawer dresser that did double duty as a television stand, and a low shelf that could be a seat or a luggage rack. The flatscreen TV was the newest thing in the room. It was not the typical accommodations of the Pictrain family, but Arthur Mark Pictrain IV was not a typical Pictrain.

Each side of the bed boasted a built-in shelf below a wall sconce. The television remote rested on one next to a plastic triangle tent bearing the motel logo that replaced the ubiquitous matchbooks and ashtrays that used to be placed there. It had the available cable channels on one side and internet access instructions on the other. Mark sighed and stood up. Hotel internet sucked.

He shuffled back towards the door, passing a small nook with a mini-fridge under a shelf that held a microwave and a two-cup coffee maker. A small basket holding coffee filter packs and a couple of foam cups sat on top of the microwave. Heading to the bathroom, Mark took an exaggerated, careful step over his bag, mocking his earlier misstep. He paused at the door to double check that it was locked and flipped the swing guard over to engage it. No one knew where he was, but it was better to err on the side of caution.

Turning on the bathroom light, he jumped at the grinding clank of the overhead fan. His shoulders slumped as he leaned forward and looked at himself in the mirror.

His narrow face looked tired, but clean. Melancholy brown eyes studied the lank hair that hung limply at his neck. "Muddy straw" Grandmother Pictrain called it. Mother would ruffle it with her fingers and whisper "chocolate chip cookie brown" in his ear whenever Grandmother passed judgement. The corners of Mark's mouth trembled.

Today it was definitely muddy straw. His polo shirt was a medium blue, grayed from frequent washing, and his khaki slacks had lost the wrinkle war. "Scruffy looking," his father would say.

The toilet continued to run after he used it and no amount of handle jiggling would make it stop. Giving up, Mark washed his hands and splashed some water on his face, scrubbing it dry with the thin, scratchy towel.

Plumping the two flat pillows together as a backrest, Mark snagged the remote and turned on the television as he settled back on the bed. He muted the sound, and after glancing at the offered channels, selected the hotel menu and just watched it scroll by in an eternal loop. The life of a traveling salesman was not a *bad* one, he continually reminded himself. He was surprisingly good at his job, and his sales area had grown larger and more profitable. The downside was always being on the road, with little opportunity to spend the money that had begun to accumulate in his bank account. Of course, Corporate was always raising his goals, pushing him to work harder and longer, because as his sales grew, so did their profits.

This was his life. Drive to the next hotel. Camp out. See clients. Enter orders. Eat, sleep, repeat.

He was a long way from Connecticut. Tilting his head back to rest against the padded headboard attached to the wall behind the bed, he closed his eyes as he imagined what his family was doing. By now they would have figured out what he'd done. After his initial outrage, Father would have passed the problem on to his top fixer, and he would be in his study, Cuban cigars within reach, watching several news and finance channels simultaneously on the three high-definition monitors on his desk. Mother, in her expensive pantsuit and pearls was probably indulging in a single chocolate martini on the patio before dinner. The twins, practically clones, would be on the tennis court or practicing their violins in the parlor. They were headed to Yale next year. Destined for all that he had left behind.

Well, he hadn't wanted that life then, and he didn't want it now. The real problem was he didn't want this life he was living either. In fact, all he wanted right now, was to wash the fatigue of the drive, the despondency of his surroundings, and the failure of his life down the drain.

Forty minutes later, skin glowing red like freshly steamed lobster, Mark emerged from the foggy bathroom, a towel around his hips. It was impressive how long the motel's hot water had lasted.

He gave the door a cursory glance, compulsively double-checking the locks, and froze at the white corner of a slip of paper that had been shoved underneath the door. Frowning, he gave it a tug. The paper moved slightly, then caught. He gave it another, more forceful tug, and the paper shifted, then started to tear. He'd have to open the door to get it.

Mark tapped his fingers against the door frame. It was probably junk. A pizza delivery, dry cleaning, or onsite car-washing service flyer that some homeless person got paid pennies to cram into every door. He didn't need it. He didn't need to know what it was. His fingers drummed as he stood at the door. Who was he kidding? It was like a splinter in the finger of his solitude. He wouldn't be able to relax until he found out what it said.

Studying the door, Mark decided that if he put his toe on the paper, left the swing guard engaged and unlocked the door, he should be able to open it just enough to drag the paper inside. He wouldn't have to get dressed; he could clear up this mystery and go back to bemoaning his life. Fine.

First, he put his ear to the door, listening. Nothing. The walls might be thin, but the steel door was almost sound-proof. Mark took a deep breath. "No one knows I'm here," he told himself, but anticipating unlocking the door had his heart pounding and his palms sweating. Wiping his hands on the towel around his hips, he positioned his left foot *en pointe* on the corner of the paper, then slowly and quietly turned the deadbolt above the door handle. Taking another calming breath, he quickly turned the knob, and yanked the door open so hard it bounced against the end of the slide bolt, nearly catching his nose. He dragged the paper inside, slammed the door shut, engaged the deadbolt, and stood panting.

He was sweaty and shaking, the clean feeling of the shower completely erased by the feral reek of fear. The cool door against his hot skin steadied him, and he closed his eyes to focus on breathing, like his long-ago counselor had instructed. In through the nose; one, two, three. Gently out through the mouth; one, two, three. Slowly, his heart stopped pounding. Mark opened his eyes. Another shower would be nice, but when he bent over to snatch the paper, a wave of vertigo left him staggering. The aftereffects of the adrenaline surge. Keeping his left-hand trailing along the wall, he walked to the dresser, turned, and with two quick steps, collapsed on the bed. The towel he was wearing dis-lodged as he fell, leaving him naked, face down on the questionable cleanliness of the comforter.

Inhale, two, three.

Mark coughed at the musty smell he'd sucked in from the fabric. He pushed himself up and realized he was shivering as the stinky sweat dried on his clammy skin. Moaning like a wounded animal, he stood and yanked back the covers, sliding in between the rough sheets, and curling himself into a tight ball with the bedding and pillows packed around him.

As his shivering subsided, Mark realized he still had the paper from the door crumpled in his hand. He thought about wadding it up further and throwing it across the room but the curiosity that felt like it had nearly killed him just opening the door wouldn't let him. He clutched it to his chest until he felt warm enough to sit up, reposition the pillows as a backrest, and turn on the bedside light.

Smoothing out the wrinkles against his legs beneath the bedding, Mark began to read.

> Mr. Pictrain,
>
> My apologies for this intrusion, but in the brief time you've been our guest, we have had numerous calls to your room that went unanswered. After several unsuccessful attempts to reach you, the following persons requested that we hand-deliver a written message with their phone numbers, asking that you contact them as soon as possible. Please call the front desk if you have any questions.
>
> Melissa Ridgeway
>
> Guest Relations

Three names and numbers were listed below the message. Erin Martinez, his Regional Sales Manager, and boss. Jimmie Creed, his booking agent, and Arlen Morgenstern, the chief of his father's security division.

Mark shuddered as he read the final name, and slid down under the covers, as if they could protect him somehow from the all-seeing eyes of Morgenstern. Despair congealed in his stomach, and he wanted to be sick. How had they found him? Only Erin and Jimmie knew he was coming. Huddled in the blankets, Mark considered his options. He could ignore the calls, but he couldn't ignore the fact that his father's security team had located him just a few days after his last visit home, when he should have been a needle lost in the haystack of highways across America.

Sighing, Mark slid out of bed and grabbed his duffel. Thunking it down on the desk, he dug through the outer pocket and pulled out his cell phones, one for regular work and family, one for his real life. He switched them both on, and while they powered up, he pulled out clean clothes; a plain white t-shirt and plaid pajama pants. Collecting the phones, he climbed back into bed.

Regular phone first. Several missed calls. His mother. His father. His boss. The security chief. Only two had left messages. The first was from his boss, Erin. He scanned the text transcription and grimaced.

> Mark, I tried to reach you before you checked in, but you weren't answering. I'm sorry, but I'm going to have to put you on suspension. I've been informed you are facing felony theft charges. We can't have you representing our company to our clients until this is resolved. I'll cover the first night at the hotel since I couldn't reach you, but only one night. Call me when you have cleared up this issue and we'll put you back on the

circuit. You're a great salesman. I don't
want to lose you. Good luck.

He rubbed the spot between his eyebrows with his free
hand and let his head fall back against the wall. "Felony
theft charges." Great. That was Morgenstern's work. Mark
tapped the next voicemail, the one from Arlen Morgen-
stern. Short and blunt. "Call me before this gets out of
hand." He closed his eyes, his thoughts rolling back to that
last evening at home.

His father, Arthur Mark Pictrain III, had decreed a formal
sit-down family dinner, so everyone was present, pressed
and dressed in their best, which for Mark, was a sport coat
over his polo shirt and slacks.

His mom and sisters, three shades of blonde: ash, honey,
and platinum, wore various versions of the classic black
cocktail dresses, with matching strands of pearls. His fa-
ther's black suit might look unassuming, but the trained
eye would recognize the quality of the fabric, the precise
tailored fit, and the expensive gray silk shirt, paired with a
custom burgundy power tie.

They took their usual seats, the twins flanking his father,
continually competing for his favor, while Mark sat on his
mother's left hand at the opposite end of the table. As
they decorously dined to the subtle tings of silver on china
through the salad course, the soup course, and the entree,
Mark's father dominated the conversation. He grilled the
girls on their studies, their after-school activities, the re-
ports he'd been given on their social media presences. He
critiqued Mark's attire, the way he was wasting his talents,
and hinted that if he showed proper remorse for his bad
choices, he could come back home. That there might be

a position available in the family business. Entry level, of course.

After dessert was served, Father reached into his jacket, pulled out a velvet box, and placed it on the table. Mark's sisters lasered in on it, but his mother gave an almost imperceptible sigh. With a flourish, his father opened the box and lifted out a diamond-encrusted necklace. Holding it up and letting it dangle from his fingers, it transformed the light from the chandelier into brilliant sparkles that flickered across their faces. A single strand of round diamonds increasing in size from the clasp to the inch-long pear cut pendant in the center. Fire and rainbows danced around the room as the breathtaking teardrop twined from his father's fingers.

Stephanie and Elizabeth leaned in, their mouths open, mesmerized by the magnificent money twisting slowly in front of them. His mother looked down at her plate, her hands in her lap. Mark couldn't keep his eyes away from the necklace. It was captivating. Beyond stunning. The glittering brilliance pierced his soul, awakening a lust that shocked him with its intensity. He wanted to hold it, to feel the cool stones slip between his fingers, to cradle the pendant and stare into its fiery depths. The desire was so strong he found himself clenching his hands together under the table to keep from reaching out to snatch it.

Confident he had everyone's attention; his father began speaking.

"This necklace has been in my family for three generations. Your generation will be the fourth. The question is, which of you will be worthy of receiving it?" He tilted his wrist, giving the necklace more movement, sending more rainbows around the room. He turned towards his daughters. "Perhaps one of you could earn it through outstanding achievements at the university." He turned toward Mark. "Or perhaps even you could earn it, by settling down and producing the next heir in the Pictrain line." He smiled at Mark coldly, then looked at Mother, sitting quietly. "After all, that's how your mother earned it." He stood and walked down the length of the table to stand behind his wife. Draping the necklace on his wrist, he brushed her hair aside and undid her pearls, letting them fall into her lap. He opened the clasp on the diamonds and brought the strand down over her face and around her throat. Settling it around her neck and securing it like a collar, he lifted her hair back into place. Bending down he brushed a kiss against her cheek, patted her shoulder and headed to the parlor for his after-dinner drink and cigar.

The twins jumped up and scampered after him, eager to learn what achievements Father might consider worthy of winning the prize. Mark sat quietly, watching his mother. As the silence lengthened, she looked up at him and gave him a small smile. She reached behind her, undid the clasp, and laid the diamonds on the table. She stood up, her pearls in her hand.

"Be true to yourself, Mark."

Head high, Juliana McIvy Pictrain walked out.

It was just him, the half-eaten desserts, and the alluring jewels. He reached over and touched the pendent with the tip of his finger. An electric shock ran up his arm straight to his heart. Against all logic, he wanted that necklace. Had to have it. Impulsively he stood, dropping his napkin on the table, coincidentally covering the diamonds as he scooped them into his palm. Slipping his hands into his pockets, he left the room, readying an excuse for departing immediately rather than in the morning.

* * *

Whump. Whump. Whump.

Mark banged his head against the padded headboard behind him. What had come over him? If he'd just taken one moment to think. He knew his father would never let that necklace just disappear. He had all the pieces of his life working in sync. Why had he screwed it all up for a piece of jewelry?

Flinging back the covers, he stomped over to his duffel. Angrily he unzipped the top and fumbled around inside, feeling for his dress shoes. He pulled a wadded stocking out of the toe and opened it, unveiling the puddle of sparkling light in his palm. He licked his lips. Just seeing it again, he felt that same soul-deep longing to hold this beautiful item, to feel it against his skin. He closed his fingers over it and shut his eyes. If he was going to lose everything he'd built over *this*, then at least for tonight, he would own this necklace.

Suddenly determined, he straightened, then remembered he hadn't checked his other phone. Sure enough, the pay-as-you-go phone had two missed calls with voicemails, both from Jimmie Creed. His voice was quivering with excitement in the first message. "Call me! You won't believe it! I have great news, but I gotta tell you in person. Call me." In the second message, Jimmie's excitement was tinged with panic. "Seriously. Call me ASAP! I need to KNOW if you are going to make the show tonight. Someone special is going to make a guest drop-in. You will RUE it if you don't call me, and I will be a-PAUL-ed. CALL ME."

Mark dumped both phones on the bed. Jimmie's teasing hint sent tingles of excitement down his spine. Tonight could be his big break. Morgenstern's terse message had cold shivers cascading over him. Tonight might be his last show. Either way, he needed to prepare before he returned any calls. He'd proven it in his sales career. People could sense your emotional state over the phone. If you stood, you came across more powerful, strong. Dress to impress, and your confidence transmitted down the line. For these conversations, he needed to be his absolute best self. Time to armor up.

Mark took great care with his ablutions. Paying attention to every tiny detail of his grooming: shaving, moisturizing, trimming and cleaning his nails, combing his hair, brushing and flossing his teeth. Then the transformation he lived for. Silk panties and a lacy corset with compression and padding in all the right places. Thigh high stockings, silk of course. His father had given him an appreciation for fine clothing. He fussed over his makeup, wanting a more natural appearance rather than the exaggerated colors and contours normally required on stage. He strapped on the black stilettos that had taken him months to learn to walk in then shimmied into the sequined black sheath dress, his favorite because it reminded him of the chic black dresses his mother wore most often. He looked at his reflection in the motel mirror. Hip cocked, his right foot on its toe, his leg parting the side slit that ran way up his thigh. He tilted his chin thoughtfully, wondering if the sequined dress would cheapen the diamonds. No. The low sweetheart neckline would be perfect. The diamonds would elevate everything else. Satisfied, he lifted his wig into place, and brushed the golden waves that fell just past his shoulders.

At last, it was time. Tingling with excitement, he lifted the necklace from its sock wrapping and laid it against his chest. The cool stones burned like ice on his skin. Flushed with exhilaration, he closed his eyes, and reached under his hair to fasten the necklace. Slowly, he let his fingers glide over every stone as they came back to the front, caressing the teardrop, then smoothing his every curve all the way down. Heart racing with anticipation, he opened his eyes. Gasped softly. They were perfect. Beautiful.

She coquetted in front of the mirror, turning and twisting, letting the sparkle of the stones delight her from every angle.

Now she was ready. After a few selfies, she would call Jimmie to let him know she was coming. She'd tell him to make sure he took lots of photos of her performance tonight. Tomorrow Morgenstern would find her. Take back the beautiful diamonds, threaten her and humiliate her. But that was tomorrow.

Tonight, she would follow her mother's advice. She would be true to herself.

Blowing a kiss to her reflection, Marvelous Miranda held her head high and strutted out to meet her future.

Valley Terrace Island

DIANA RECKART

One. One single match in the matchbook that Alex had found in the boat's wreckage. It was sealed inside a plastic bag and stuffed in a duffel in one of the cupboards. Other than that, there was not a lot salvageable from the ship that had run aground in the storm.

"Stupid, stupid, stupid," he kept muttering to himself. "Stupid for going on this trip, stupid for going on the boat when a storm was brewing…" He scrounged around in what was left of the tiny cabin, jerking open the cabinets and drawers that remained intact. "…and stupid for telling myself I could go alone!" Rummaging around he found a water-logged map, some zip ties, a length of rope, and some fishing line to join that lonely matchbook with only one stinking match left in it. That was it. There was no signal beacon, no additional compass, and the only flares he could find were soaked to the point of being useless. The match was the only hope he had of getting help. "Who saves one match in a plastic bag?" he muttered again. "Stupid, stupid, stupid."

The morning started out bright and sunny. Robinson and Alex planned on renting the small sailboat for a day trip. Alex really needed time to decompress. Life had gotten a bit rocky, so his brother and he had taken a vacation to get away from it all. Their second day, Rob, as he preferred to be called, made a suggestion.

"Why don't we take a day to sail around the islands? It'll be just what you need," he assured him.

Alex enthusiastically agreed. They made it down to the dock and rented the boat when Rob got the inevitable call from work.

"It's called VACATION, Hunter!" The elder brother was doing his best to keep from screaming over the phone. "Can't Taylor handle this contract?" He shook his head in disgust at the answer.

Rob had been much more successful in his endeavors and at life in general. While they had both earned business degrees, he had made better decisions on how to apply his. Starting out on the ground level for a national company, he had recognized some market opportunities, quit his job, and delved into those investments. Now, he was the owner of multiple businesses. As great as that was, work frequently interfered with play.

Alex turned away and gathered up his stuff in preparation for the cancellation of their outing. It was probably a good thing anyway. Liquid gold filled the sky now, but the forecast warned of a looming storm. Regardless, their plans were made so they had ignored the warning, brashly believing that they had the sailing ability to maneuver ahead of any bad weather before it became an issue. Rob observed Alex packing up while continuing his conversation.

"Look, I can head back to the hotel and get on the conference calls there." He looked at Alex, regret shading his eyes as he continued the phone conversation. "But I am going to expect the team to be able to handle this after today." He ended the call abruptly.

"Alex," he began apologetically, "we got to call this off for today, brother. Duty calls!" Rob scowled. "Yeah, just can't find good help nowadays, uh, present company excluded, of course!" He laughed half-heartedly.

Alex winced at the remark. His own forays in the business world had been blatantly unsuccessful. After college, he ended up working in a local company that went belly-up. He tried his own business venture, but it never yielded the income he needed to sustain himself. Rob "rescued" him with a job opportunity. But while Alex thought he was good enough to get into the inner workings of one of Rob's businesses, instead of giving him a position in the company hierarchy, he relegated him to selling cars at his dealership. Brotherly love didn't mean much in this family.

Oh boy, Alex thought to himself, *I bet he thinks I can't do this on my own.*

"I think I will go for it anyway...you, know, Man against the Sea." Alex was firm in his response. A desire to show Rob that he was quite capable seethed inside and made him commit to the trip, even though doubt about the sail was percolating in his head "You do realize that you're going to get stuck on the phone all day, right?"

"Yeah...probably true. Well, if you really want to do it, good luck with your adventure," Rob called as he hurried away to deal with business matters, "Don't go too far; that storm won't stay away forever." His brotherly concern evaporated with every step. Alex started to answer with a witty retort, but his sibling was already back on his phone before he even had time to respond.

And so, he began his endeavor, determined and excited. He'd do a solo sail and demonstrate his mettle, setting off on the small boat that was manageable for one. It handled easily enough as he navigated out of the small harbor and into open waters. Once exposed, without the shelter of land, wind buffeted the craft, but Alex maneuvered without any major mishap.

Columbus has nothing on me! he thought jubilantly. He was amazed how much the taste of the salt breeze and the caress of sunlight erased his worries.

Cutting across the open sea, he sailed until he was past any visible land. Excitement and joy overwhelmed him as he reveled in the freedom he now felt. It was only when the sleeping monster appeared on the horizon that doubt entered his mind. It was obvious that he needed to turn the boat around and head in.

The arms of the storm were creeping over the edge of the water, dark and ominous, reaching across the sky to snatch away the golden day. As the blackness grew, he raced back to shore, but the monster swelled until it trapped him in its furious grasp, pulling him far out to sea. In the darkness, the wind and waves nearly toppled the boat. He fought valiantly, hanging on desperately to the rudder and trimming the sails when he could, but the storm flung the vessel about. It wrestled the controls from him as the jib tore and the force of the storm took over the steering. After it dragged him towards some outlying islands, it finally cast the vessel aground, shredding it against the rocky shore.

As fortune would have it, Alex was thrown from the deck, missed the rocks, and landed in a sandy dune. Half-dazed, he lay there and let the rain pelt him until the storm passed and a few rays of that once promising golden light reappeared.

Now, here he was. Alone, on an island, no telling how far out.

And it was all his own fault.

Another failure.

He shut his eyes. *Why him?* But there was no point in sitting around feeling sorry for himself. His instincts and survival mode kicked in. The day was escaping. Now that some of the sun's rays managed to sift through the murky sky, they were no longer gold but amber, signaling his limited time to work. He needed to do what he could before he lost the light. His first step was to search along the shore to find some rocks. After throwing enough of them in a pile, he assembled an "S" and then an "O" and another "S."

"Maybe there's enough light for a plane to spot it tonight. At least it will be ready for tomorrow," he muttered aloud. "If anyone is even looking."

His next move was to check out his surroundings. The island didn't appear to be too big. He estimated he could probably walk its circumference in a day. There were lots of trees and bushes, which was a good thing. After venturing into the flora, he dug in the undergrowth for some wood for a signal fire. The storm had soaked a lot of it, but enough had stayed dry enough under the protection of the brush to make a decently sized pile. He dragged it down to the beach. Using almost forgotten Boy Scout skills, he stacked the wood for a small bonfire. His job wasn't done.

He headed back several times until he gathered enough to stoke the pile.

Once he was satisfied with his signal preparations, he sat down in the sand and pulled out the matchbook again. A logo with "VT" graced the cover. Valley Terrace and the phone number were written at the bottom of the front. Based on the inner cover, it looked like a multi-use facility, touting a variety of amenities. "Henry VIII" caught his eye. That was apparently the name of their bar.

I could use a good stiff drink now.

That reminded him of the small water container on the boat. He ignored it in his search for rescue materials. After retrieving it and seeing its minimal contents, the realization struck him that there was a good chance of running out of water. There were rainwater puddles on the rocks, so he dug around the wreckage some more until he found an empty water bottle and a piece of hard plastic that could fit under the surface of the puddles. Painstakingly scooping water, he managed to almost fill the bottle. Task completed; he lay face down to drink from one of the pools.

"Phfshet!!" he exclaimed as he spit some of it out. The sediment from the rocks made it a less than refreshing beverage, but without knowing how long he would be marooned, he figured he better take advantage of the resources he had. Fatigue made his arms and legs ache, so despite the lack of time before nightfall, he trudged slowly over to a soft spot on the beach to collect his energy,

Alex lay there, and closed his eyes. Reality nagged at him every moment. His muscles ached from the fight with the storm and his clothes, wet with rain and sweat, clung to his skin. He wondered if a search party was sent out yet. And then he wondered if they would even bother. It wasn't like his brother would miss him. He pulled out the match-book again. A signal fire was probably the best chance he had of being found. He laughed to think that his life might depend on this one little match. There it was. Right in the middle of the book. He found it funny that someone would pick matches evenly from both sides until this one was left smack dab in the middle. A thought occurred to him. *What if the match doesn't even light?* The matchhead looked intact, but he knew all too well that appearances could be deceiving. After all, look at him. Ivy league college-educated, brilliant, responsible, and yet he was selling cars in his brother's business. Not exactly the fireball he had hoped to be.

He turned his attention to the striker. A match was no good without a way to ignite it. This striker was well-worn on the right side. *Must have been a left-handed user* he mused. It cast another doubt as to whether the match would come to the rescue. Was the striker too worn? He began to wonder. Was that his issue? Did he lack the spark to make his life a success? Maybe it was bad luck. Maybe he just didn't have the right game plan to be as successful as Rob. Or maybe it was the way others looked at him. Maybe his past failures led to the conclusion that he wasn't capable of any more, similar to his own assessment of the matchbook. Did his first failure condemn him to a life without success? After all, here he was, needing to be rescued.

Or did he?

He gave the inside cover of the book another look. It listed restaurants, the availability of fuel, and a host of places to be entertained. Food, shelter, and entertainment.

That's all you really need to survive, right?

He wondered as he around some more. The island seemed lush enough. There were materials to fashion a shelter. He bet there was some edible vegetation as well. Even if there wasn't, he had the fishing line and he was a pretty decent angler. There was bound to be something in the wreckage to serve as a hook to supply himself with protein. The region was typically pretty wet. He bet it would rain enough to give him what he needed in fresh water.

Maybe I don't need rescuing.

The match could start a fire not as a signal beacon, but as a way to cook and keep warm. Once a fire is started, it just has to be tended for it to stay alive. Surely after time, he could become adept at starting a fire without a match. The thought turned over and over in his mind.

He looked out at the water. Was that a ship on the horizon? His heart beat wildly. Craning his eyes into the dusk, he saw tiny lights in the distance. The object slowly got bigger. Were they searching for him?

It was time to light the fire. It was time to be rescued. Staring back at the ship, he saw specks he thought could be people on the deck.

Turning his attention to the island, a surprising disappointment filled him. What an adventure he could have! What a survival success he could be!

He looked at the pile of wood. He looked at the match.

Okay, match. Time to get lit.

He looked at the ship.

He looked at the match.

He looked at the island.

There was really only one thing to do.

After tearing the match from the book, he held it up high and stared at it. His heart and mind raced like a stampede of a thousand horses.

He took a deep breath quieted himself into a gentle rhythm. Speaking with utmost calm he said, "Okay, Match, here's the plan."

The Corrected Legend of Convict Hill Bar & Grill

A J JINKINS III

Austin, Texas has long held a reputation for being a bit…well…eccentric. Matter of fact, one of its citizens' favorite mantras is "Keep Austin Weird." So, it should come as no surprise that, while striving to maintain such a lofty reputation, facts often get muddled with local folklore, urban legends, and municipal myths when it comes to factual representation. Such is the case involving one of the Texas capital's most historically beloved eateries, which comes to mind merely because I find myself flipping the matchbook cover bearing its name open and closed out of nervous habit as I await the arrival of my devoted companion for the evening. We are not meeting at Convict Hill Bar & Grill. The establishment in which I find myself this evening is new, modern, with a retro disco vibe that has sadly found its way back into today's pop culture, though many have lamented that disco and all of its accoutrements should stay dead and in the past. My eyes are drawn to the simple matchbook cover that I relentlessly fiddle with. Long nestled within the deep breast pocket of my tweed "stuffy-old-writer jacket," as my lovely wife calls it, I must have picked these matches up decades ago and forgotten about them until this evening when I discovered the memorable treasure as I was searching for my pen.

Convict Hill Bar & Grill. Just on the outskirts of the sprawling city, off of a two-lane highway illustriously named 290, this Austin classic is a diamond in the rough, an Austin tradition, to coin a trite cliché which any writer of quality knows is in poor form. From the street, the structure appears to be a large log cabin style farmhouse, but upon closer inspection, it becomes obvious that the rough-hewn log look is simply a false veneer added in an attempt to give the drab, dated building a bit of character. The cheesy façade is belied, however, by the alluring aroma of quality southern fare. The smell of smoked beef, a seared T-Bone steak, sizzles as the waitress walks by and sets it proudly before the cowboy at the next table. The sweet scent of a triple-something chocolate-laden dessert resting half-eaten before a stuffed-tick momma. The mashed taters swimming in the brown gravy that will not be saved from drowning because, "It's just so much." The endless conversations of businessmen and congressmen, children screaming in delight as they are set free from the table to run about the place, touching the coarse fur of the stuffed animals that, over the years, have been donated by hunters with nowhere to display them at home, as if they were exhibits in a petting zoo. Feet sticking to the floor either because of years of wax or maybe spilled food that didn't quite get cleaned up well enough. Though I was a much younger, stronger man the day I procured the matchbook in my fingers, I can vividly recall, as I linger in longing for my familiar date to appear, some of the various tales of how the place came to be. Now I will commit another heinous act of writing taboo by addressing you, the reader, directly and endeavoring to educate you on the true history of Convict Hill Bar & Grill, and once finished, you will be edified, content in knowledge that the facts, being what they are, have been made clear and free from contestation.

Given that a large maximum-security prison, Texas' largest business by far, was erected in the early part of the last century atop a mesa-style plateau merely a half mile from the restaurant, it would be a quite simple mental jump, or rather, a skip, to conclude that the place was named in honor of the institution. Convict Hill could rightly be the title the locals had given the compound. Certainly, when the eatery first opened so many years ago, the prison was about the only thing out that far, and the state employees would have made up a majority of its customer base. This is the version that the lazy accept as truth concerning Convict Hill Bar & Grill. It requires little imagination and even less thought to accept this explanation and move on about life, dismissing the simple logic as unimpressive, not worthy of more consideration.

But there are other possibilities floating around out there, hovering over Lake Travis like the fruit of a tree, just out of reach of the mundane but accessible to those who stretch or dare to climb for it. One such possibility claims that Convict Hill Bar & Grill was named so due to the fact that nearly every felon released from the prison—having been locked up for years or even decades, and being let out with nothing more than their bag of commissary-purchased possessions and a check for, back then, $50—would inevitably stop off there to cash their parole check and get their first real meal before heading back into the city to start over. Thus, the moniker Convict Hill Bar & Grill. This explanation requires a tad bit more romanticism in one's personality and may be abhorrent to those who favor the simple facts over more fanciful imaginings.

The correct version of the legend of Convict Hill Bar & Grill—whose name I have spelled out eight times, thereby creating what is known in writing groups as an "echo" and is generally frowned upon, especially by my wife, Laura— challenges the mind as well as the senses. I have already provided the olfactory, tactile, and savory aspects of the restaurant as well as the visual and auditory lack of appeal the building offers. The time has arrived that I compel my- self to relinquish my knowledge to you in the matter of the moniker of Convict Hill Bar & Grill.

Convict Hill Bar & Grill is not called "The" Convict Hill Bar & Grill. The modifier "The" is not in the name. It is simply, "Convict Hill Bar & Grill." The story behind the rea- soning will clarify any confusion you might be experiencing right now.

You see, back in the early part of the last century before the restaurant was first opened, the original proprietor, a young woman by the name of Lucinda Hill, was desperately in love with a young man, Colt, who claimed to be a wealthy rancher. Now, wealth was not all that important to Lucinda. She would have loved Colt even if he didn't have two nick- els to rub together or a pot to piss in and a window to throw it out of. This was fortunate for Colt because, as it turned out, he was, as they say in Texas, all hat and no cattle. Now, Lucinda had not been out of her own back yard much and, growing up without her mother, who died in childbirth with her younger sister, she was in no way wise to the ways of the world. Being pure and virtuous, and thoroughly naïve, she and Colt wound up becoming overly familiar one evening and Lucinda became with child.

Well, long about Lucinda's third month, her father, Lucky Hill, became aware of her condition and vowed to avenge her honor by killing the man who fathered the baby. Lucinda refused to turn Colt over to her father, claiming she did not know the father's name as it was in the dark of night and the stranger had caught her unawares.

Meanwhile, Colt was experiencing some troubles of his own. Seems he had swindled a couple of prominent businessmen in the Austin community and now the law was after him. When the Rangers finally nabbed him, they held a trial within two days, and Colt was found guilty and sentenced to 25 years without parole. Lucinda Hill was allowed to visit him, which she did every chance she could. Every time she turned to leave Colt after her visits, she would hear the prison guard say, "Come on, convict."

Oh, here is where it all comes together. When Lucinda Hill's baby was born, a bouncy boy with blue eyes and golden locks, she knew she could not name him Colt because that would tip off her father as to who had put her in such a way. She thought about how she could honor the father without risking his life and eventually came up with the idea of calling him Convict. So, the boy's name was Convict Hill. Colt, upon hearing about his son and, beaming with the pride of all new poppas, told Lucinda where he had stashed the money he had stolen. She found the loot right where he said it was and immediately bought the building where Convict Hill Bar & Grill still stands.

And my date has just arrived, so I must go now and be weird. I'll just put this matchbook back right where it was. What is this? I will educate you concerning the other matchbook I just found in my pocket on another occasion.

Flight Ticket

DIANA RECKART

Bustling into the nearly empty bar, Brenda began her Tuesday night shift with a disappointed sigh. Her shoes stuck to the dirty floor, making a tacky pop as she walked past the worn chairs and cracked tables. She surveyed the nearly empty room. Business would have to pick up a lot more if she was going to fill her tip jar. Volume was the secret since the scruffy patrons of this establishment were not overly lavish with their gratuities. She put up with enough pawing and leering from men who had no good intentions to end up with pittances for her service, but that was her reality. Working two crummy jobs was not the way she hoped to spend the rest of her life. She hoped...for a lot of things. Mostly she hoped for a way out of this going nowhere life in this middle-of-nowhere podunk oil town.

After running a damp cloth along the counter, she stacked glasses and dusted the bottles of spirits. Snorting to herself, she thought about the hidden personalities and closely guarded secrets the colorful liquids had the power to reveal. The human drama that unfolded before her eyes every night felt like the same old rerun on perpetual replay.

After an hour or so, business did pick up. A few of the regulars came in; husbands escaping their wives or men who had no other place to go after a long day in the field. There were also a few roughnecks that she didn't recognize, probably rotating in from some other god forsaken hellhole to service the facilities in the oil patch. There were always a few females hanging around too. Women looking for a little excitement or some guy to buy them drinks in exchange for some attention and whatever else they were willing to hawk. Brenda spent a couple of hours delivering foamy glasses of beer and shots of tequila, rewarded by unwelcome pats on her backside and leering looks at her ample bosom. Thankfully, her tip jar was fuller, but it was far from what she needed to pay all the bills.

After making another sweep of the tables, she went behind the bar and started washing the glasses that had begun to stack in precarious towers by the sink. Her heavily mascaraed and fake-lashed hazel eyes rolled slightly as she realized they were like her own pathetic life, a crystal tower that could crash and break at any moment.

And then it happened. After years of just the same-old-joes walking in through the door, he came in. HE came in. Tall and broad-shouldered, the virile stranger headed for an open spot at the bar. His head of raven hair was trimmed neatly and his face just started to show traces of a five o'clock shadow. He wasn't dressed in shining armor, but she already wondered if this was her knight. Could he be her ticket out of here? After all, he wasn't the usual customer for this rundown joint. His clothes and demeanor showed he was way too high-class to be frequenting a dive like this.

She began to wonder if he had lost his way trying to find the much ritzier High Desert Lounge. As he drew close, Brenda caught her breath ever so slightly. Her heart skipped a beat when he took his seat.

He tossed his pack of cigarettes and matches on the counter. "Scotch, please. Chivas, if you've got it, Johnnie Walker if you don't."

Brenda was taken aback. His deep voice took her to the depths of the world and back. "I am afraid Johnnie Walker Red will have to do. Sorry about that." She added an alluring tone to her voice as she apologized for the selection.

He looked into her hazel eyes. She saw a twinkle of understanding in his. "That will be fine."

"Do you want it on the rocks or neat?" The heat in her eyes increased with every second she looked at him.

"Neat for me," his gaze moved over her face and across her chest. His glance stayed there just long enough to appreciate the view, but not long enough to be crude.

She poured his shot on the back bar so he wouldn't see her tremble. Inhaling a calming breath of air, she steadied herself as she set his glass in front of him. It did not pass her notice that his ring finger was empty and lacked the tan line she saw on so many men's hands. He grabbed his drink, breathed in its heavenly vapors, letting its heady aroma tease his senses. He tilted the glass and let his lips embrace the drink. After rolling it in his mouth, he gently swallowed. Putting the glass back down, his gaze wandered around the room.

Brenda shook herself out of her trance and grabbed a tray. She quickly moved around, bussing tables and checking on orders for seconds, thirds, or fourths. She made sure she was all the way across the room before she let herself look at him again.

There he was. This magnificently tall, she guessed 6'2", man with dark hair and long legs. His face was a throwback to the movie stars of the 50s with a strong jaw, Greek nose, and startling eyes. She loved the broad shoulders he carried under his jacket and the apparent strong chest muscles that rippled beneath his starched white button-down shirt. There was just little bit of a belly that protruded over his belt, but Brenda found that forgivable considering the rest of perfection he presented. Judging by his expensive clothes and his taste in scotch, she figured he was some rich oil man who might be her means to escape the drudgery that trapped her.

He sat there, sipping his drink and savoring it like a scarlet sunset. She savored him with every glance she could steal. Finally returning to the bar, she leaned forward, maybe just a little too far.

"Are you in town for a visit?" she asked.

"Business," he answered quickly. His eyes already caught hers like a magnet, "But I like to have a little fun too!"

A shiver went through her. She allowed herself to imagine him aiding her escape.

Before she knew it, he grabbed his glass and cigarettes, got up and headed out to the patio where the smokers were. Her heart sank, afraid he'd find another spot, or another lady. Forcing herself to cut her losses, she got her mind back on the job and went about tending to the other customers, hoping desperately that there was still an opportunity to grab his attention.

Once his nicotine desires had been sated, she was delighted to see him head back to the same seat. He motioned for her to come over for a refill.

"Will you be here long?" she asked as animated as she dare.

"Long enough. I've got some meetings to go to and some sites to visit." He took another measured sip of his scotch. "Then I hope to have an afternoon or two to play. I've got a single engine Cessna to toy around with. Thought I'd take if for a few spins."

"Ooh, that sounds like fun!" Brenda hoped she didn't betray her eagerness.

"Hey, Brenda, I'm empty down here!" One of the regulars was banging his glass on the counter.

"I'm coming; hang in there." She hurried off to fill his glass. A few more customers caught her attention and she was forced to make another round through the tables before she could get back to *Mister Take Me Away from Here*.

He seemed deep in thought when she got back so she ignored his half-full glass and asked if he wanted another. He chuckled. "I'm still working on this one. Make sure it doesn't run off while I use the facilities." She nodded as he got up and headed to the men's room. While he was gone, she looked at the cigarettes and matches he left on the counter. The smokes were the usual lung-sooting brand that most oil men smoked. The matchbook intrigued her. Window Petroleum Company was printed in red and blue. A silhouette of North America bore a tiny star at the company location. She grabbed it and flipped it open. Perfect. A blank inside gave her just the opportunity to write her name and number on it.

While she was at the taps filling an icy mug with the watery lager the regulars always ordered, he came back to his seat. After delivering the frothy libation to its anxious drinker, she looked over to see if he noticed the matchbook, which she had deliberately cracked open with her number visible. Glass in hand, he grabbed the matches and stroked his thumb across the handwriting. A wry smile crossed his face and he glanced down the bar in her direction.

His gaze made her blush, something she hadn't done in years. Her shaky feet carried her back to the spot in front of him. She gave him her best smile and hoped he couldn't tell how fast her heart was beating.

"Want to go for a ride?" he asked.

"A ride?" She was guarded, not sure if this was innuendo. Hoping he didn't misunderstand her attentions, she continued, "What kind of ride?"

"In my plane. Remember the Cessna?"

"Oh, your plane!" She laughed nervously. "Of course, I remember. I've never been in a plane before; you must be pretty smart to be able to handle that." She stared into his hypnotic eyes and drowned in their pale blue depths.

"Smart enough. I have meetings tomorrow until three. Can you be at the Johnson private terminal at M-O Central Airport at four? That should give us plenty of time for a flight before dark."

Batting her false eyelashes at him, she answered, "I'll be there," and trotted off to tend to the other customers.

* * *

At a quarter to four, Brenda, wearing her best white K-Mart capris and a cherry red halter topped by a light denim work shirt, walked into the small terminal at M-O Central

Air Terminal. She had never been to a private terminal and was surprised by the high quality of the furnishings. There was a desk with a neatly coifed attendant and a coffee bar with snacks. Some patrons sat waiting in lounge chairs while others fixed their gazes on laptops at a sidebar. The whole place smelled clean and new. She settled into one of the seats facing the entry door and waited. "Reese." She said it softly to herself as she waited for him. He shared it with her last night as he finished off his drink. Even his name exuded the rich quality that she was pursuing as her ticket out of her pathetic life.

At one minute to four, he strode through the door. He no longer sported the jacket, but still wore a crisply-pressed button-down shirt, blue this time. She couldn't understand how his khaki pants didn't show a single wrinkle. His physique, or at least what she imagined it looked like under the confines of his clothes, still made her heart race.

He acknowledged the attendant and then sauntered over to Brenda.

"You ready for some fun?" he asked with a grin.

She stood up next to him, her tiny frame dwarfed by his stature. The scent of some fancy men's cologne enveloped her.

"Whenever you say," she answered with her best smile.

He led her out the glass doors that opened to the runway. They had to walk several yards down to the hangar, all the while passing Lear jets and Cessnas parked on the side of the tarmac. He stopped next to a white single engine plane with blue running stripes.

"Here's our chariot," he said as he opened the passenger door for her.

Glad she had opted for some simple Mary Jane flats instead of heels, she climbed onto the footstep and then into the seat. The small cabin space made her feel a bit claustrophobic, but she calmed herself by thinking of the opportunity it presented.

Reese walked around the plane, presumably performing an inspection. Once he finished that task, he jumped in and nestled himself in the pilot's seat. He went through a few more checklist items and cranked up the engine.

Brenda could feel the adrenaline course through her veins as they taxied to the runway. Having never flown before, she was excited, nervous, and scared all at the same time. She found herself holding her breath, glad that he was apparently too focused on his flight checks to talk.

Arriving at the end of the runway. He wheeled the plane around, turned to her, and asked, "Ready?"

She nodded quickly. He throttled up the engine and hurtled them down the straightaway. At first, Brenda felt like she was riding in a freight train going full speed when all of a sudden, the wings lifted and the ground released them from earth. She felt elation in every fiber of her body. The ground moved farther and farther away as they rose into the deep blue sky and the terrain changed before her eyes. Trees and shrubs became mere dots and the ground became a multi-colored palette. She couldn't believe how quickly everything shrank away below her.

Reese leaned over and looked at her face. "Fun?" he asked quickly, his voice raised over the drone of the engines.

"It's thrilling! I can see why you like it." Now she couldn't tell if her excitement was from the plane ride or being with him.

He climbed high over the desert until they leveled out. The town slipped away as they explored the world above the ground. Wisps of clouds slipped past them as they journeyed on. Eventually, he tipped the wing to turn the plane, making her stomach rise and filling her with an intoxicating experience. He was just pointing out some landmarks when a CLUNK interrupted them.

"What was that?" Brenda asked while trying to mask her nervousness. She looked at Reese who had lost all the color in his face. The engine started to sputter and he exclaimed, "Oh, sh—"

Brenda grabbed her seat arms. Terrified, she looked at him for comfort.

"What's going on," she asked, almost in tears.

He didn't answer her. His knuckles were pure white as he gripped the controls. A panicked look was pasted across his face. He babbled, "Oh, no! Oh, no!"

Now she was really scared but sanity took hold of her. The engine continued to falter but Reese sat there, immobilized. She felt like she was watching a bar fight, which prompted her into action.

"What are you going to do?" she screamed at him.

He slammed his hand against the steering yoke. "What the hell!" Suddenly his face went from ash white to beet red. Beads of sweat formed across his brow and a litany of expletives poured out of his mouth. As far as Brenda could tell, he wasn't taking any action. He was locked in a chasm of anger.

The engine sputtered and started to slow down. She knew enough about cars to know they were almost to the point of no return. And then...the engine died.

"Do something!" she yelled.

Finally, he came out of his daze. He nosed the plane down and cranked the engine. It chugged at first but restarted, mercifully delivering them from an untimely end. Brenda breathed a sigh of relief as the angry color drained from Reese's face.

"I think we need to cut our joyride short," he said shakily. Turning the plane around he headed back to the airport. Then it happened again, the terrifying sound of the engine sputtering.

Reese yelled. He looked like he would boil over again. Brenda couldn't believe her eyes.

"Come on, Reese," she pleaded. She grabbed his chin and jerked his face toward her. "You know what to do. Get us back to the airport."

Shaking her off, he nosed the plane down again and cranked the engine. Luck was with them, it started again. He grabbed the radio and hailed the tiny airport control center. "M-O Central, this is November-five-niner-one-one-whiskey, over"

The radio crackled and the flight controller answered leisurely, "November-five-niner-one-one-whiskey, go ahead, over."

"Mayday, mayday. Engine trouble." Reese stopped and swallowed hard. "Heading back for M-O Central. Advise. Over."

The controller answered, his voice no longer relaxed but all-business, "November-five-niner-one-one-whiskey, you are clear for runway. I'll move all traffic away. You are good for approach."

Reese could hardly keep his hands on the controls they were shaking so much. Brenda was shaking too, simultaneously furious and incredulous that her life lay in his hands.

They limped back to the airport. The engine failing over and over again, forcing them to dive and restart. Each time, Brenda watched as Reese was snared by anger and she had to snap him into action. At one point, he looked down and saw a smooth stretch of desert sand.

"Maybe we should ditch it there..." Reese said seething.

Brenda held back the words she really wanted to use and firmly encouraged him, "Go for the airport. If you can keep the plane running, I think it's better if we try for that."

After what seemed an eternity, the airport was in range. The engine sputtered one more time, repeating the terror, with Reese restarting it again before they began their final approach. Brenda hoped if all else failed, at the very least, he'd be able to glide it in. At this point, she half wondered if she shouldn't take over and do it herself.

The runway finally came into view. Flashing lights could be seen in the distance as emergency vehicles lined up at the end. Brenda prayed their luck would hold long enough to make them unneeded. Reese angled the nose for the approach and they descended; as slow as eternity. Closer and closer the earth came. Brenda watched the ground and Reese, hoping he wouldn't explode during the approach. She let out a big breath when the wheels finally hit the runway. He pulled the plane all the way to the end of the strip before they stopped. Once he shut the engine down, he opened the cockpit door and jumped down to the ground. Airport personnel came running up, high-fiving him and landing walloping pats on his back, a hero's welcome.

Brenda watched all this as she took a moment to stop shaking and to say a prayer of thanks for making it safely. Grabbing her purse, she unsteadily climbed down to the ground. After taking a long look at the handsome rich man...she headed straight for the parking lot.

The Last Soldier

LAURA JINKINS

A shield-shaped outline encompassed the words "Wood-lawn Country Club" and "Mount Vernon Virginia," snuggly framing a silhouette of George Washington surrounded by laurel branches. It was an elegant colonial design for a lowly book of matches. The edges of the cover were worn, the dark green top layer of paper with the yellow logo peeling away to reveal the white core. A recent member of the club had left it on the table, along with a very chintzy dollar tip.

The waitress scooped the matchbook up with her tip and headed out the backdoor for her break. Standing beneath the rear exit awning, she flipped the book over and over between the fingers and thumb of her left hand, tapping her last cigarette on her thigh with her right. Judith hated working at the country club. Her smoke breaks were markers that got her through her shift until quitting time. The members were full of themselves, dressed in their golfing attire during the day and their dinner attire at night, arrogance oozing from them like biscuit dough from a busted can.

She placed the Salem 100 between lips in need of another swipe of Ruby Red Revlon lipstick, which had been removed by her most recent cigarette butt—that butt now tumbling somewhere downstream in the gurgling gutter wash of an earlier rainstorm. She opened the book of matches. Three. Three matches left. Two more than the number of cigarettes she had, so she guessed it would be okay. When she smoked this last one, she was going to quit. Really.

The three paper matches with white phosphorus heads stood at attention, awaiting orders. Pulling the first match from the trio, she closed the book carefully and held her breath while dragging it across the striker. It hissed, sizzled for a split second, and went out—a ghostly thin tendril of smoke taunting her. She cursed quietly around the cigarette dangling between her lips. Tossed the spent match on the ground. Looked intently at the remaining two.

She hated matchbooks. They were always hard to use, the thin strikers wearing out long before those on sturdier matchboxes. *Beggars can't be choosers*, she thought. The matchbook was her means to closing the door on a decades long habit. She would smoke this last cigarette, *really* enjoy it, and then be done. She wouldn't buy any more Salem 100s; she wouldn't think of a mostly used matchbook as part of her tip. She told herself she was worth more than that. She was worth fresh smelling hair and clothes, white teeth, and lungs that didn't rattle when she had to hustle during the lunchtime rush. She craved the ability to say "no" to the habit as much as she craved the cigarette.

Almost.

Judith couldn't remember when she first started smoking—her early teens? She'd been smoking for so long, it seemed like she'd followed her afternoon milk bottle with a cigarette and a nap. Had there been a time when her clothes, her hair, her breath hadn't smelled like a dirty ashtray? A time when her fingernails didn't have this yellow tinge? If there had, she couldn't remember it. A recent development, though—a nagging cough that refused to go away—had finally gotten her attention. And so, this was her last hurrah, her final cancer stick before she went to the doctor and was formally told, "You have to stop. You're killing yourself."

Grasping Soldier #2 from the cardboard comb, she held it firmly and prepared to ignite it. "Come on!" She struck the match and struck out again. "You. Have. To. Be. Kidding. Me!" she spit out through teeth clamped around the cigarette filter. When she lit up her first cigarette years ago, she practically gagged on the smoke filling her virgin lungs. Smoking was a habit that had helped her fit in with the other kids who hung out behind the high school stadium, and the habit had continued long after she needed the nicotine more than she needed those friends. Now the monkey was firmly attached to her back.

She took a deep breath, stretching her abused lungs as far as they would allow, then let it out. Pulling the last match from the book, she tried to relax. Eyes closed, she steadied herself, opened them and then ordered the last soldier to fire. The white tip hissed and burst into flame. She quickly cupped her hand around the cigarette and held the tiny bonfire to the tip, drawing the flame through the tobacco. The end of the cigarette glowed red, and she sighed as the nicotine began to travel through her body with each puff. "Finally."

Tension eased from her body and she relaxed the vise-like grip she'd exerted on the filter, holding the cigarette loosely between her lips. Suddenly, she was wracked by a violent hacking cough, so forceful she bent forward, hands on her knees trying to catch her breath, tears squeezing from her closed eyes as she tried to clear her chest. The spasm passed and she opened her eyes.

Looking down, she saw her last cigarette floating in the rainwater puddle next to her feet.

The Source of the Spark

JENNIFER SIMS

The stiff brown bag gives a crackle and pop
It is rough, gently worn in my hands, and filled
A matchbook collection, ready to swap
Their stories are ripe for a writer's guild

We grab some matches and though we don't know
We dream up their past and how they got here
What adventures were had decades ago
Remembered by a matchbook souvenir?

We gather together, eight members strong
Sharing our words, those both written and told
A diverse mix of views but all belong
Respect for each and the name we uphold

Thank you for reading all our matchbook prose
We hope you enjoyed what we have composed

About the Authors

Lynnette Brooks Asked about what kind of writing she likes; Lynnette will tell you poetry. It suits her love of all the good things in life: family, friends, nature, pets, and the ocean. In her younger days she was an avid scuba diver, world traveler and wildlife rehabilitator. This will be her first venture into the published word. Lynnette's current project is learning to live with her new status as a widow. Poetry covers that too.

A J Jinkins is a displaced island dweller who loves the Gulf Coast, writing, and music. When he has time off from teaching school, he attempts to master the art of surfing and devotes his time to several community efforts such as running a helps ministry, Hope For Homes, which brings people together to aid homeowners in need. AJ and his lovely wife live in a tiny rural community just a few miles away from the beach. AJ's goal in writing is to honor God and his family in every endeavor. He has published several short stories in local magazines.

Laura Swan Jinkins has been in love with the written word since toddlerhood when her mom kept a legal pad list of all the books they read together. Reading led to writing: poetry, short stories, freelance magazine articles, and a novel in progress that her friends emphatically demand she complete. Other loves: her husband, AJ and their daughter and son-in-law, as well as the sweetest granddaughter ever. She enjoys needlework, scrapbooking and antiquing for mid century china and glassware, as well as running her small window coverings business.

Diana Reckart is an adoring grandmother, avid church volunteer, continuous improvement professional, and half marathoner. An excerpt from her fantasy novel, *Virtuosity Village* was a finalist in the 2021 San Francisco Writers conference contest. She is currently working on a memoir recalling the incredible story of her grandmother's flight from the Mexican Revolution and her grandfather's rise from a copper mining worker to the first Hispanic lawyer to pass the Arizona Bar.

Corinna See is a writer and an unpublished novelist who spends her free time "drinking ink" — that is, reading as many books as possible, and (at least thinking about) writing. She has two bachelor's degrees, one in creative writing and one in French, both from the University of Houston. Find her at home with her husband and the love of his life, a red heeler/Lab mix.

Jennifer Sims is a chemical engineer who spends her free time reading, practicing yoga and Pilates, and drinking her two favorite beverages: coffee and beer. She's dabbled in creative writing since taking a few courses in high school and has just enough tools in her writer's toolbox to be dangerous. Jennifer hopes to spend more time writing once she finds a break in wedding planning. She currently lives in the Houston, Texas area with her soon-to-be husband.

Kathy Sims is a retired chemical engineer, and obsessive reader. She lives on the Gulf Coast of Texas with her husband, (also an engineer), occasionally dodging hurricanes, but mostly swatting mosquitoes. She enjoys writing stories that look for the quirky possibilities in life.

Titles by Author

See, Corinna

Spats
The Illness Next Door
Faye
Suburbia Inn

Sims, Jennifer

The Source of the Spark

Sims, Kathy

Humphrey's Oasis
Rendezvous
Super 6 Motel